SAINT JC SOUTHWORTH

OF

SAMLESBURY

1592-1654

HIS LIFE AND TIMES

Glen Clayton

I would like to extend my grateful thanks
to all who have helped to produce this booklet.

Glen Clayton © Copyright AD. 2017.

The right of Glen Clayton to be identified as the author of this work has been asserted in accordance with the Copyright, Designs and Patents Act, 1988.

ISBN 978-1-5272-9893-4

CONTENTS

LIST of ILLUSTRATIONS   Page 5

THE MAIN PROTAGONISTS & FACTIONS
OF THE TIME   Page 7

INTRODUCTION   Page 9

CHAPTER I: John Southworth's Early Years: 1592-1637.
           Page 12

CHAPTER II: Political and Religious Battles: 1638-1653.
           Page 32

CHAPTER III: Reverend John Southworth:
July 1653 onwards.   Page 83

APPENDIX.   Page 100

Douay College.   Page 100

The Alumnus Oath.   Page 100

The Oath of Allegiance.   Page 100

The Oath of Abjuration.   Page 101

Extract from the 'Basilikan Doron' by King James VI,
(Ed. Jas. Craigie).   Page 102

The Book of Common Prayer.   Page 102

The Petition circulated during the plague of 1636.   Page 102

Saint John's Last Speech.   Page 105

John's Divided Family   Page 108

Problems at Samlesbury Higher Hall after the First Civil War.
                                       Page 112

Oliver Cromwell and the failed Republic.   Page 114

Richard Cromwell, the Second Protector.   Page 118

BIBLIOGRAPHY.   Page 123

ILLUSTRATIONS

Sketch map drawn up for Lord Burghley: HM state papers MPF1/123 c1590: Front and back cover.

St. John in Westminster Cathedral: Front cover: Photo by kind permission of Anne Marie Micallef, (co-ordinator of the Guild of Saint John Southworth, Diocese of Westminster).

Charles I, by Gerrit Van Honthorst, reproduced by kind permission of the National Portrait Gallery. Page 15

Queen Henrietta Maria: artist unknown, reproduced by kind permission of the National Portrait Gallery. Page 17

The pony skin trunk c1600-1630, found in Samlesbury Hall: Page 21
Photo from *Staging the World: Shakespeare:* J. Bate & D. Thornton.

Page 19 of *The Popish Royall Favourite,* by Wm. Prynne. Page 23

John Southworth's letter to Queen Henrietta Maria. Page 29

Copy of Francis Windbank's warrant, 1640. Page 34

A 1644 Five Shilling piece of Charles I. Page 41

Prince Rupert by Gerrit Van Honthorst, reproduced by kind permission of the National Portrait Gallery. Page 43

The first published portrait of *Cromwell,* by R.S., 1647, courtesy of the National Portrait Gallery. Page 51

Map of Battle of Ribbleton Moor. Page 61

A mark inscribed on the boulder in Brockholes. Page 62

Some of the *musket balls* found in Samlesbury. Page 63

Execution of Charles I, courtesy of Purnell Books.
(Kings & Queens).   Page 77

A 1658 Half Crown of Oliver Cromwell.   Page 78

St. John Southworth: Portrait by John Trinick, 1890-1974,
Fellow of the British Society of Master Glass Painters,
which is based on a photograph taken after his coffin was opened in
1927.   Page 91

Plan of Discoveries at Douai.   Page 93

Relic at Samlesbury R.C. Chapel.   Page 98

Statue of St. John Southworth under a replica of the infamous triple tree of
Tyburn: St. Mary and St. John Southworth's R.C. Chapel, Samlesbury.
(Photo, S. Jones).   Page 99

The slab of Portland stone which marks the site of Tyburn gallows,
(set on the traffic island at the entrance to Edgeware Road,
near Marble Arch): By kind permission of Tyburn Convent.
                                                  Page 106

Inscription in the Heythrop book: photo by Fr. Charles Newdigate, S.J.
                                                  Page 107

A doodle from the Heythrop book, bearing St. John's initials.

THE MAIN PROTAGONISTS & FACTIONS OF THE TIME

There were **three** main schools of thought within the **English Churches** in 1647:-

Anglicans, who adhered to Episcopal government;

Puritans/Presbyterians, who were extreme Anglicans adhering to a Presbytery. They opposed church rule by Bishops and most morphed into Independents.

Independents – the Non-Conformists who leaned to a wider liberty than that afforded by Bishops or Presbyters.

The **four** main parties within **the State** in 1647, were:-

Royalists, who supported the monarchy unreservedly.

Moderates who were mainly Presbyterians and had no quarrel with the King; but looked for limited political, constitutional and religious reforms.

Independents who agreed more with Presbyterians, although on different terms. They fought the First Civil War for the radical reconstruction of the Church and State and the dawning of a new age of Godliness. Most became republicans.

Levellers who were political – social revolutionaries whose principles were similar to communists. They considered that Cromwell and his colleagues had not gone far enough – in addition to abolishing the Established Church, they wanted to break down all distinctions of rank, birth and class. By the summer of 1647 they were a growing force in the New Model Army, the third faction after the Presbyterians and Independents.

By 1646 there were **five parties** in **Ireland**, each with its own army:-

The **Irish** Confederates under Owen Roe O'Neill.

The **Scots** under Monro.

The **English** Royalists under the Duke of Ormonde.

The **English** Parliamentarians under Coote.

The **Papal** force directed by Rinuccini.

INTRODUCTION

Over the years a considerable number of Samlesbury parishioners have served in the Ordained Ministry, including many Southworths, but Saint John is the most well known.

By the time he was born (c1592) England had survived the worst years of hostile offensives from Philip II of Spain, the Papacy and Cardinal Allen[1] – who had each tried, but failed to eliminate Elizabeth I.

Spasmodic conspiracies, however, were continued by Philip III and Guy Fawkes, who was executed for the Gunpowder Plot which failed to blow up Parliament in 1605. These ongoing machinations were the cause of intense suspicion and distrust within the Government – if the schemes had been successful, Spain would have ruled England and Roman Catholicism could have been imposed on all. One of the defensive measures introduced were the Penal Laws, which were extended and rigorously enforced whenever necessary.

Despite all this, intensely devout young men – many of them sons of the gentry – were still being urged to flout the law, by studying for the priesthood at one of the English seminaries abroad and then returning to England to bring the 'heretics'[2] back to the Roman Catholic fold. New seminarian priests were urgently wanted to reinforce and, in time, replace the 'old' recusant priests, who had been particularly successful at keeping

---

[1] Rev. E.E. Reynolds: *John Southworth Priest and Martyr.* Allen was related to many of the Lancashire gentry & visited most of the great Catholic families in the county, (1560-1565), exhorting any lapsing Catholics to desist from attending their local parish church, as Pope Pius IV, (& later his successor, Paul V), had declared the 'schismatic' Anglican Services to be unlawful. Allen later trained for the priesthood, established an English training college for the English Mission at Douai, (1568) & was in league with the King of Spain & Papacy against Queen Elizabeth.

[2] Those who rejected the established doctrine of the R.C. Church and did not recognize the authority and infallibility of the Pope. At the trial of the *'famous witches of Samlesbury'*, Thomas Potts commented, *'For they are Heretics accursed, to leave the company of priests, to frequent Churches, hear the word of God preached, and profess Religion sincerely.'* (Recusants were those who refused to attend the Church of England, as required by law).

Roman Catholicism alive in Lancashire[3]. It was a dangerous undertaking, but John Southworth was one of those who responded to this call from Rome, (although several members of his family had already conformed to the Anglican Church[4]).

The 17th Century was a particularly complicated time. Not only did questions and problems revolve around the various Christian denominations, but also around the Constitution:-

- What was the relation between Crown and Parliament?
- What were the rights and duties of the King?
- What was the function of the Houses in government?

The **Royal position** was that England should be ruled, (as it had been for centuries), by the wisdom and skill of its monarch, supported by Church, ancient law and chosen counsellors, financed and advised, but not controlled, by Parliament.

Members of Parliament were determined to become partners, rather than mere advisers. They considered that they were equal in wisdom, skill, authority and – by virtue of the ancient right to vote taxation – even superior. In 1407 the Crown had conceded that any bill appertaining to finance had to have its origins in Parliament; so, although Charles believed in absolute monarchy, they were already influential and finance was usually the reason for a Royal summons.

The House of Commons was a petitioning body, whilst all legislation required the consent of the House of Lords.

It was *'the raising of money by un-Parliamentary taxation and [his] efforts to enforce uniformity in the church, [which] combined to rouse the animosity of both Puritans and men of property',* towards Charles. They also disliked the King's foreign policy, (which the sovereign had

---

[3] Christopher Haigh: *Reformation & Resistance in Tudor Lancashire:* By 1584, 1/6 of those who trained at Douay had come from Lancs., where an early recusant Burnley schoolmaster, (who later taught at Blackburn Grammar School), recruited at least 9 young men for the seminary at Douai.

[4] Potts, 1613: *The Wonderfull Discoverie of Witches in the Countie of Lancaster:* and J.Southworth & A. Dudgeon: *A History of the Southworths of Samlesbury, 1300-1890.*

always directed), and the favour shown to Roman Catholics. A compromise appeared impossible, but in recognizing that the Crown headed both Church and State, Parliament had also recognized the hereditary principle, which automatically added weight to the sovereign.

Oliver Cromwell and his colleagues considered that the Reformation did not go far enough. They were intent on the destruction of the English Church establishment – particularly those practices which seemed to reflect Roman influence. It caused years of scandalous, chaotic upheaval, both political and religious – the British Civil Wars, the execution of a King, a 'Commonwealth' and a military dictatorship.

Saint John Southworth lived through it all and this account is an attempt to explain how those horrifying events led to his execution in AD.1654.

CHAPTER I

JOHN SOUTHWORTH'S EARLY YEARS: 1592-1637

Oral tradition asserts that Saint John Southworth was born at the Lower Hall of Samlesbury, Lancashire[5], during the reign of Elizabeth I. It is unclear where he fits into the Southworth's extensive family tree, but he is believed to have been a grandson of the third Sir John Southworth, who was manorial lord between 1546 and 1595.

Although nothing is known about Saint John's schooldays, in 1592 *Dingley*, (an apostate priest and government intelligence agent), reported that a recusant schoolmaster had been living at Samlesbury Higher Hall for the previous ten years. So it would appear that there was at least an elementary education available in Samlesbury, before the young people moved on to a higher education elsewhere. This may have been at Blackburn, because W.A. Abram, (*History of Blackburn*), states that back in 1567 Sir John Southworth had become a founder governor of Blackburn's new *'free gramer Schoole of Queene Elizabeth,'* and sometime between 1585 and 1590 he, *'his tenantes and followers,'* together with his son, Thomas Southworth Esq., collectively contributed £30-6s-8d. towards the augmentation of the endowment.

Sir John was also one of the Lancashire gentlemen/clergy[6] who sponsored aspiring students through Oxford or Cambridge. So although Sir John [3] was religiously conservative, he appears to have been quite amenable to others being exposed to alternative

---

[5]Bishop Ric. Challoner, (1691-1781), mentioned the Samlesbury connection in his *'Memoirs of Missionary Priests'* and took his information from the collections of *'Mr. Knuresborough, [1672-1724], and other memoirs in my hands, and from a manuscript sent me from the English college at St. Omer's.'* It was also he who fixed John Southworth's year of birth.

[6] Haigh: (Alexander Nowell of Read, Lancs., who became Dean of St. Paul's, was particularly generous to students who attended his old College of *Brasenose*).

ideas and making their own decisions, even if they were different ones to his own.

PREPARATION for MINISTRY:

When he was twenty-one, (1613), Saint John entered the English Secular College in Douai as a convictor[7] and took the College Oath[8]. Being well qualified for the course, he had no need to do foundation studies, (Loffler) and doubtless he had read at least some of the recusant books in Sir John's library.

As was customary at the college, John took the precaution of adopting an alias, which the Douay Diary records as *'Lee'*. This is believed to have been his mother's maiden name, so perhaps Nathaniel Lee – a recusant yeoman in Samlesbury in 1580 – was a close relative. (There were still some *'Lees'* in the parish in the 18th and 19th centuries).

John received the tonsure in 1614 and took the Alumnus Oath, (see p.99), in December 1615 – promising *'in due time'* to return to work in England, which was *'now afflicted with heresy.'*

In April 1616 rumours were circulating that some of the college staff and students believed that the Oath of Allegiance (p.99) to King James I could lawfully be taken, so they were each asked to submit a statement of denial. Father A.B. Purdie says that all signatures were *'subscribed in the presence of an Apostolic and Public Notary,'* but John was not present, so *'signed separately, the rest of the company bearing witness that he had written his name with his own hand.'*

A translation of John's declaration reads:- *"I, John Lee, call God to witness that I do not think otherwise about the Oath of so-called Allegiance than the above think, that is, that it is erroneous, damnable, execrable, and involving open perjury, and I also execrate Widdrington's opinion. Nor do*

---

[7] *The Third Douay Diary*, Catholic Record Society, Vol. X. One supported by private means, ecclesiastics, family, or friends. It was hoped that the families persuaded into recusancy would provide sons, shelter and money for the seminarians. (Those who didn't have private means were called alumni & were supported by papal pension).

[8] Rev. A.B. Purdie: *'The Life of Blessed John Southworth:* Students had to recite the Creed, promise to keep the college rules and do nothing to disturb the observance of its discipline.

I know of any supporter of that opinion in this College." The Latin declarations were forwarded to the Pope, who declared himself satisfied and *'the college was entirely cleared of the calumny.'*

Purdie comments on *'the old troublesome question as to how far a Catholic admitted that his allegiance to the pope could free him from allegiance to the civil power under which he lived, or how far he was ready to allow the one to over-ride the other. Unhappily, the Catholics were unable to ease the minds of critical enquirers on this point…As a body, they were frightened off the question by the unsympathetic attitude of Rome and the English public was left to draw the only natural conclusion.'*

The Douay Diary says that John returned to England on 3rd May to convalesce and it is true that there was much sickness and a high mortality rate at the college – students were sometimes advised to eat in town, and both Purdie and Whitfield point out that the buildings were ruinous, deficiencies extant in many areas, (including diet and finance), and students were inadequately clothed.

But was he sick? The Southworths were Lancastrians, loyal to England and the Crown and their tenants were usually the only ones fully armed at the military musters. John was young and may have felt uncomfortable about submitting the above declaration; he certainly expressed a very different opinion at his execution:-

"…So I say that if any Catholics should offend the law and not show themselves true obedient subjects, let those that offend be severely punished…the Catholics of this nation who are natives of this land…are as true subjects to his highness and this present government as it stands established, as any Protestant of this nation of what degree soever[9]*…"*

By the time John returned to college ten months later, plague[10], which was a huge European problem, had broken out in Flanders and was spreading to Douai; but the College escaped infection and he received Minor Orders in 1617, was ordained

---

[9] Westminster Archives (XXX,635). Also Purdie, p.123.
[10] Rev. N. Schofield & Rev. G. Skinner: *St. John Southworth, Parish Priest of Westminster.*

on Easter Eve 1618, completed his studies and then spent some time with the Benedictines. (Long-term bickering between the Seculars[11] and Jesuits on both sides of the Channel was distasteful to many and caused some to test their vocations in other Orders; but John returned to the Seculars).

EUROPEAN ALLY by MARRIAGE TREATY?

James I had begun looking for a powerful European ally and, despite strong objections from Parliament and much of the populace, between 1618 and 1623 he spent time negotiating a possible marriage between his son Charles and the Roman Catholic Spanish Infanta. The penal laws were less rigorously enforced and at the end of July 1618 the Spanish Ambassador had secured the release of sixty priests, who exchanged imprisonment for *'perpetual banishment.'*

Bishop Challoner notes that John was sent on the English mission in October 1619 and apparently worked in London, *'not without profit.'*

There was great joy amongst the Roman Catholics, when the Bishop of Chalcedon became Vicar-Apostolic of England in 1623. Briskly he set to work and soon established a Dean and Chapter and John readily subscribed to their authority.

---

[11] Seculars were Diocesan priests, subject to a bishop and Jesuits were monastic, subject to an abbot. Purdie writes that this widespread dissension was felt even in an Order of Benedictine nuns, who were under the spiritual direction of the Seculars.

At that time there must have been considerable freedom of worship, because on 26th October, some three hundred Roman Catholics were able to gather in an upstairs apartment in the French Embassy and listen to a renowned Jesuit preacher. Tragically, their combined weight caused the collapse of the floor and it crashed through the lower storeys, killing about ninety persons. Most people in the neighbourhood rushed to help and King James immediately sent his condolences, but some fanatical Puritans were a disgrace to mankind, throwing mud and stones at the dead and injured. (Purdie).

The marriage negotiations, however, failed – Philip IV of Spain and the Pope had been adding *'increasingly unworkable conditions into the marriage treaty'* and there was still a very real fear of European and Papal dominance. When Charles returned home without a wife there was national jubilation and the Puritan-dominated Parliament demanded the re-enforcement of the Penal Laws. *'Roman Catholic clergy,'* they said, were the *'professed engines of Spain and the laity a body of traitors.'* A proclamation was issued *'that all missionaries should be banished [and that] the lord mayor should be commanded to arrest all persons coming from Mass in the houses of foreign ambassadors....'*

On the advice of Dr. Kellison, the President of Douay, John returned to the college in March 1624 for a *'year and some months'* and spent part of the time as a temporary confessor to the English Benedictine nuns in Brussels. (Whitfield).

SUCCESSFUL NEGOTIATIONS

Meanwhile, King James was negotiating another marriage treaty for Prince Charles – this time with Henrietta Maria, Madame Royale of France. Orders were given for the release of all those imprisoned for religion and many recusancy fines were re-imbursed. (Purdie).

Charles acceded to the throne in March 1625 and married his Queen Consort, fifteen-years-old Henrietta Maria, in May. Because she was a practising Roman Catholic she was never crowned and *'she refused to defile her beliefs by attending his coronation*[12].*'* Despite this, it was agreed that she would have priests and freedom of worship in her own personal chapel at St. James's Palace. In addition, on their wedding day Charles ordered the relaxation of the English penal laws, (which caused great offence in Parliament).

Whilst the marriage gave England an important ally, the King could not control his wife – she was proselytising and regularly interceding for imprisoned Roman Catholic priests. It was difficult for him to maintain a balance between her and his Puritan-dominated Parliament, which was angry, anxious and suspicious about her ever-increasing influence[13].

Before long, searches for priests and religious items were vigorously resumed and in 1626 Charles deported the Queen's household.

---

[12] Trevor Royle: *Civil War.*
[13] Royle & Reynolds: (One of the queen's chaplains – George Leyburne – was a student at Douay during John Southworth's final year and later became President of the College).

IMPRISONMENT IN LANCASTER CASTLE

Saint John appears to have returned to England in the summer of 1625 and may have worked for a time in the north, because it was in Lancashire that he was arrested in 1627 – the safest and most Catholic county in England. Many gentry were religiously conservative and determinedly adhered to the Church of Rome, whilst their secluded country manors – already the local administrative centres – naturally became the local Mass centres. One such mission, (dedicated to Saint Chad and in use until 1818), was at the Lower Hall of Samlesbury and ran in conjunction with another mission across the river at Higher Brockholes, although, according to folklore, it was sometimes necessary to hold Mass and Baptisms secretly in the woods around Bezza.

The manors were widespread and often ran contiguously, so it was possible for priests to travel through many miles of countryside in comparative safety. In an easterly direction, for example, there was a central band of Roman Catholic estates running from Samlesbury and Hoghton, through to Blackburn, Harwood, Church, Padiham, Burnley and Colne, accounting, in 1604, for 144 of Blackburn Deanery's 183 recusants. Local officials frequently adopted a 'live-and-let-live' policy and in 1592 there were believed to be ninety-three households within the county where seminarians could find shelter and help. The recusants operated an active, well-organized network, which was vital to the movement – *'runners'* carried messages, news or warnings between families and *'lesser men'* acted as guides to priests unfamiliar with the county. If necessary, says Reynolds, priests could lie low in the wild moorlands, fells and forests, and this also hampered law enforcement. In addition, an effort was made to marry off the young people *'within the faith.'*

Only 42 (out of approximately 145 priests/seminarians believed to have worked in the county), are known to have been arrested, whilst recusants from Durham, (1577) and Yorkshire, (1595/1600) – plus five of the six priests who escaped from Wisbech Castle[14] in 1600 – were all kept safe in Lancashire.

So John probably fell foul of an informer and his trial took place at Lancaster. He was condemned, but, because the King had promised that no priests would be executed solely for their ministry, he was granted a Royal reprieve. A pardon, however, was not forthcoming – that would have needed Parliamentary consent. (Reynolds).

It would appear, though, that John had been allowed at least sufficient freedom to exercise his ministry, because it is recorded that he was *'very well esteemed of by Catholics'* at Lancaster. Certainly attitudes towards the prisoners had been very relaxed in previous years; e.g., in 1592 there were complaints that detained recusants were *'allowed to go hunting, hawking and racing and even carried arms in the streets of the town*[15]*'* and six years later the Bishop of Chester made a similar complaint, adding that the *'notorious abuse of law & justice should speadily be reformed'*. In 1600 Richard Cowling S.J. wrote that, in Lancashire *'Catholics are so numerous that priests can wander through the villages and countryside with the utmost freedom.'*

John was still at Lancaster Castle in 1628, when he was joined by Father Edmund Arrowsmith. He too was a Lancastrian and had studied at Douay before John arrived. Edmund is believed to have said Mass at *Lower Hall, Fleetwood Hall* and *Church Bottoms* in Samlesbury and at *The Straits,* near the Samlesbury/Hoghton boundary. He had been captured on Brindle Moss, refused to take the Oath of Allegiance[16] and consequently sentenced to death for high treason at the Summer Assizes. A third priest was also in the prison at that time – a Benedictine named Edward Barlow. He administered the last Sacraments to

---

[14] Haigh: One was Christopher Southworth, a relative of St. John's.
[15] Haigh: from Salisbury MSS XI, 123 & Calendar of State Papers, Domestic, (1598-1601), 14 & 15.
[16] Brindle Historical Society & J.A. Myerscough: *A Procession of Lancashire Martyrs & Confessors.*

Edmund, but when a *'Roman Catholic gentleman[17]',* (identified as John Southworth's father), visited him, he was arrested and brought to trial. Fortunately Mr. Southworth managed to give a satisfactory reason for being in the prison and the case was dismissed.

Challoner says that, as Edmund passed through the castle yard on his way to execution, Saint John *'shewed himself out of a great window [and Edmund] lifted up his hands towards him with great humility for absolution, (for this was the sign whereof they were both agreed before), and so that priest absolved the other in sight of the people'.* (It was then realized that John's father had probably been liaising between them).

When Edmund reached the castle gates, a *'Roman Catholic gentleman'* stepped forward and embraced him *'straightly, and kissed him tenderly, till the high sheriff made him be removed by force.'* When asked to give an account of the execution, Mr. Southworth *'did sincerely protest that in the window of his chamber he saw a most resplendent brightness, such an one as in all his life he never saw before, which did show itself from the prison unto the gallows, as if it had a glistering glow, and the sun at that time was obscured with clouds, and the most part of the day likewise....'* (Reynolds).

THE PONY SKIN TRUNK AT SAMLESBURY HALL

Purdie quotes a letter, dated 8th November 1628, which says, *'Mr. Leigh,* [John's alias], *hath his apparel in which the Priest [Arrowsmith] was hung, and it is thought hath one of the quarters by this time'* and, Purdie continues:- *'These were passed by him into other and safer hands, and were the objects of much pious veneration.'*

A further extract from the letter reads, *'Worthy Sir, ...for the certainty of these things which I did deliver you at your being in Lancaster, I will affirm to be true, for the hair and pieces of the ribs I did take myself at*

---

[17] Translated from the Latin, *'Generosus'*. He was well born and the status entitled him to wear a sword and costly clothes, which were forbidden to the lower classes.

the going up of the plumbers to see the leads, when they were to mend them, and the handkerchief was dipped in his blood, at the same time of his quarters coming back from the execution to the Castle, by me likewise with my own hands. You know the handkerchief was your own which you gave me at your departure, and for the piece of the quarter, both I and some others had taken part of it for our friends, which Mr. Southworth *can witness, and that which I gave you, John Rigmaden, our Keeper [of the Castle], gave me leave to take…'*

All this was affirmed by John Rigmaden[18], Mr. Henry Holme and Thomas Thornburgh, who each certified that Mr. Southworth would be able to witness that certain relics were Arrowsmith's. Blundell also, reveals that *'the Southworth family treasured at Samlesbury many of Blessed Edmund Arrowsmith's effects')*, which must explain how vestments and liturgical items believed to have been used by Edmund Arrowsmith, came to be stored in a trunk, at the Higher Hall of Samlesbury[19]. It would be the normal practice to keep vestments etc. in 'safe' houses for visiting priests to wear and certainly these venerated items have been well used.

The trunk, (approximately 33in. x 15in. x 13½ in. high), was discovered walled-up in a first floor apartment – probably in the short, low building at the western end of the south wing, which was demolished for a large-scale extension during Joseph Harrison's restoration, (1862-1866). Edward Southworth would

---

[18] Haigh: In 1583 John Rigmaiden of Garstang was known to have given shelter to a series of priests, who said Mass in his home for the locals.
[19] Bate & Thornton: *Staging the World: Shakespeare.*

probably 'bury'[20] it when he sold his moiety of the manor in 1678.

The trunk and its contents were auctioned after Joseph's death (1880) and bought by Mr. Myerscough, whose family, (according to *Stonyhurst College Records)*, presented them to the school c1918. The pewter chalice was displayed in one of the parlours and labelled, *'The Samlesbury Chalice.'*

LONDON

There were violent scenes in the House of Commons on 2nd March 1629 and King Charles dissolved Parliament; then, with the aid of his Privy Councillors, he ruled by royal prerogative until 1640. (Oliver Cromwell, who had first entered Parliament as MP for Huntingdon the previous year, was one of the dismissed MPs and he did not forget).

It was a peaceful time and Charles, (who was obviously differentiating between his loyal, 'grassroots' Roman Catholic subjects and the political activists directed from the continent), suspended religious executions. Following a treaty with France in 1630, he authorised a second chapel for Henrietta Maria at Somerset House, together with twelve Capuchin priests and a French bishop.

This was followed by the release and *'perpetual banishment*[21]*'* of a further sixteen priests from various prisons and John was one of those transferred to the *Clink* at Southwark, prior to release in March 1630. (The Clink was a small prison near London Bridge, believed to have been in the basement or on part of the ground floor of the Bishop of Winchester's Palace, where inmates were allowed reasonable comfort and liberty, if they could afford to pay). Gaolers were open to bribes and they were particularly easy-going during the reign of Charles I, when

---

[20] It was usual to bury dedicated items when they had outlived their usefulness, to stop them falling into 'enemy' hands.
[21] Fr. JL. Whitfield: *St. John Southworth:* (CTS, 1970).

prisoners were known to mingle with other inmates, celebrate Mass, receive Roman Catholic visitors and have sermons preached[22]. (Birch, however, in his *'Court and Times of Charles I,'* Vol. I, p.96, reported a raid on the *Clink* in 1626, *'where all altars, copes, chalices, pictures, money, plate and jewels etc., were seized on and were estimated at £4,000.'* Purdie).

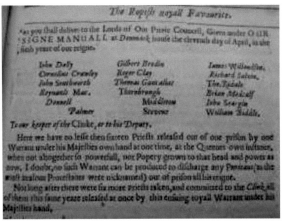

← According to Prynne's transcription of the Royal Warrant (11th April 1630), permission was given for their *'perpetual banishment'* on 24th March, when they were handed over to the French Ambassador. The Royal Warrant also states, *'That if any of them shall remaine in or returne into the Kingdome, that Our expresse will and pleasure is, That the Law should passe on every such person without further favour...'* (See indictment on p.85).

John, however, must have decided to remain in England and rely on royal influence for protection, because the Third Douay Diary records that only fifteen went into exile and Purdie notes that a month later, John was one of those who contributed £200 sterling to the English Secular clergy). It was a lot of money, so he must have had considerable financial support from his family and/or friends. John and the other donors reserved *'onely to*

---

[22] Wm. Prynne: *'The Popish Royall Favourite,'* pub. by Parliamentary authority 1643: (Prynne was a Puritan and a junior barrister, whose book was a collection of Letters of Grace, Warrants etc. of Charles & his Ministers, showing the favours & protections universally extended to Catholics).

ourselves the rentcharge thereof during our natural lives and a yeere after to be applied for the benefitt of our soules by the Deane and Chapter²³.'

By 1632 John was again in the Clink, where, according to Prynne, he *'had free liberty to walke abroad at his pleasure (as most priests during their imprisonment had, the more safely to seduce His Majesty's good subjects, and open Masses in their prisons to boote')*. Whilst there, John added his name to two Secular petitions regarding Dr. Richard Smith, (their new, titular Bishop):-

The first, (signed by twenty-four of the clergy), was sent to Dr. Smith. Following his appointment as Vicar-Apostolic of England, Scotland and Wales, (1625), he immediately ruffled feathers by exercising *'the full prerogatives of a Bishop.'* The ensuing controversies offended and scandalized many and drew government attention to his activities. After fleeing to France (1629), he spent some time under the protection of Cardinal Richelieu and was *'admonished to drop the style of Ordinary.'* So the Seculars had been left leaderless and were requesting his return.

The second letter – signed by thirty priests representing London and the eastern shires – went to Pope Urban VIII, informing him that in England *'All is confusion²⁴: there is no order, no head; scandals abound; the sacraments, especially that of marriage, are profaned; let Bishop Smith be sent back…with an authority…solid and irrefragable.'* (Purdie). This need for a bishop with full authority to settle disputes amongst the clergy was obviously very great, because the Queen and French ambassador had already forwarded similar requests to Rome.

Dr. Smith, however, continued to direct his clergy from the safety of the continent and it was a further two years before the Pope sent Dom Leander Jones to enquire into the situation. Jones found that there were over five hundred Secular priests

---

[23] Archives of the Old Brotherhood of the Secular Clergy Priests: (The established priests were trying to help their less fortunate colleagues).
[24]Purdie, Continued friction between Seculars & Regulars, (a monastic Order).

working in England, about two hundred and fifty Jesuits and approximately ten Benedictines. A second agent, Gregorio Panzani, calculated that there were 150,000 Catholics in the country but some were covert – living *'as Protestants though they were Catholics at heart'* – and keeping a priest secretly in their homes.

It was now over forty years since the attempted invasion by the Spanish Armada and almost thirty years since the Gunpowder Plot, but the priests who trained for the English Mission under the aegis of the Pope, were subject to a hostile authority from overseas and so were still considered to be potential enemies of the State. Their situation was often perilous, they re-entered England at great personal risk and muddled through as best they could, without any Episcopal guidance. Purdie says that the Seculars particularly, *'ploughed a lonely furrow, [they] were not appointed to any special sphere of work, but settled down as pleased their convenience, generally in the houses of the laity.'*
In June 1633 – eight years after his coronation in England – King Charles finally organized his coronation in Scotland. Royle comments that, unlike his father, Charles had never felt relaxed with the Scots, despite being fluent in Gaelic. James had kept the two kingdoms separate, but equal, and the Scots were currently feeling like second class citizens.

In 1635 a pursuivant, (a State messenger), named John Gray, handed a list to the Privy Council which identified thirty-two priests in various prisons around London, including *'Mr. Southworth, condemned.'* Gray complained that, although John was still officially a *Clink* prisoner, due to the liberty the prisoners had, he and they are *'all abroad out of prison…and do lie lurking in divers places within the cities of London and Westminster and the suburbs thereabout, perverting his Majesty's liege subjects, not hundreds but thousands.'* (Whitfield).

MINISTRY DURING the 1636 PLAGUE.

Although Britain kept out of the 'Thirty Years War' on the Continent, (1618-1648), thousands of English, Irish and Scots mercenaries enlisted. This troop movement was partly to blame for the spread of plague, but it also entered England via London, which was a major port and commercial centre. Many left the city as soon as possible, but others responded valiantly to the needs of the sick and dying. The King consented to the release of those held in the debtors' prisons and Anglican Church Services were shortened to limit the time people spent in close proximity with one another.

If the pest houses were full, warning notices, (marked with a red cross and the words, *"Lord have mercie upon us")*, were nailed to the doors of afflicted families and they were shut up in their homes – healthy and sick together – until the epidemic had run its course. In the parish of St. Martin-in-the-Fields alone, 1,328 people were quarantined in 324 houses. (Schofield and Skinner). Purdie says that the State Papers and Chronicles of 1636 record *'stories of heroism and cowardice, of abject terror and lofty equanimity, of loving devotion and awful neglect'*. The squalor, fear and degradation facing both victims and volunteers is impossible for us to imagine, but John Southworth had probably encountered the pestilence whilst in Flanders and would know that ministering to plague-stricken families was not for the faint-hearted.

He and Henry Morse S.J. were two of those who worked tirelessly amongst the afflicted throughout the spring and summer of 1636, but they had a rocky start when John found that Henry was administering the Sacraments of Penance and the Eucharist, but avoiding Extreme Unction, where anointing the afflicted was considered by some, to be a health risk. When Henry heard that John was complaining of his *'unworthy timidity…he discarded his apprehensions and administered to the infected all the aids of religion*[25]*'*. Fortunately, when he did contract the disease, he proved to be a natural survivor and soon recovered[26]; but for a time John shouldered the whole of their work. During September, public collections were taken and the monies distributed to plague victims in London and Westminster by the Lord Mayor. The following month the King ordered a National Fast *'to propitiate the anger of an offended heaven'* and John and Henry found their funds running out. Consequently, they sent out an appeal for financial assistance – a printed circular, describing *'the greatnesse of this calamitie [which] exceedeth all belief'*. They would never, they said, have imagined how bad the situation was, if they had not seen it with their *'owne eyes and daily experience'*. They also recounted how they were assisting over fifty afflicted families, many on the *'brinke of despaire. [Even some who] were well-born and bred [were] shut up within the bare walls of a poore chamber'*, insufficiently clothed and on the point of starvation. Others were just in need of *'ordinary helpes and remedies with which they might easily escape death, and be cured*[27]. *The example of the Protestants,'* they continued, *'both in the Citty and the Countrey, (which is well knowne to all) may bee no small inducement unto Catholicks.'* (See p.103)

Their appeal was immediately successful and over eight hundred gold crowns were collected – five hundred from the Queen – and it enabled them to administer relief throughout the winter.

A 'VAGRANT' PRISONER

Meanwhile the Rev. Robert White – an Anglican curate from St. Margaret's, Westminster – had also been working amongst the 1636 victims. He reported to Archbishop Laud of Canterbury,

---

[25] Foley's Records, Series I, quoted by Purdie. (Henry Morse began his training at Douay, joined the Jesuits (1624), then returned to England. He refused to take the Oath of Allegiance, was imprisoned for 4 years and then deported.

[26] Survivors were in the minority – if a flea bite from an infected rodent is left untreated, it can infect and kill in 24-48 hours. If it spreads to the lungs it can be passed on to others via the coughs and sneezes of the victim, but this was not known in the 17th century.

[27] Bubonic plague has a 50%-70% mortality rate and pneumonic plague 90%-100%; *'...ordinary helpes and remedies*' could not cure the sick and without modern antibiotics, the majority died.

'how dangerous a *Seducer this Southworth, alias Southwell, was [and how] ever since the beginning of this grievous visitation in Westminster, [he had] observed two popish priests to frequent Westminster, one of which is called Southwell,* " Southworth," *who is, and long hath been a prisoner in the Gatehouse[28] but lives about Clerkenwell[29]. This man,'* he wrote, was going *'in to divers visited houses in Westminster,'* distributing alms from the Queen's priests, *'and other papists,'* and converting the occupants to Roman Catholicism on their deathbeds. Afterwards, he said, he *'doth fee the Watchmen and other poore people thereabouts, that they should affirme he comes onely to give Almes...'*

Mr. White also expressed his concern that *'divers poore'* were watching with the dying and then attending Mass at *Denmarke-house*, [Somerset House], where they might infect the Queen.

So, Prynne says, John was again *'apprehended, indicted, arraigned, and the premises fully proved against him by sundry witnesses....'* State papers record that he was then in prison between 1636 and 1640, but Prynne shows him to have been a *'vagrant'* prisoner, whilst George Conn, (papal agent to the Queen), reports that *'Southworth was accustomed to say mass at his house[30]...'*

Another complaint, (similar to Mr. White's), was lodged with the Privy Council in March 1637 by Mr. Hayward, on behalf of the Rector, churchwardens and constable of St. Giles-in-the-Fields. It resulted in the arrest of Henry Morse, but he did not admit that he was a Roman Catholic priest, so the court ordered him to be deported to Belgium. (Purdie).

---

[28] Reynolds and Archer: This prison was opposite the west door of Westminster Abbey and run on similar lines to the *Clink*. One of the papers collected by Knaresborough states that when John 'did time' there, he had a *'silver key to get out and exercise his priestly ministry;'* ie. money changed hands. A Gatehouse prisoner in 1628, said that there were 15 incarcerated in the upper wards, 5 were priests & 7 were papists; the Keeper allowed priests *'daily intercourse,'* Mass was said on Sundays & Holy Days and anyone could attend, on payment of an entry fee.

[29] Reynolds: mention of 'Clerkenwell' would be of concern to the authorities, because 10 Jesuits had been arrested there, at the Jesuit *'college'* (1628) and a further plot was suspected.

[30] G. Anstruther: *The Seminary Priests*: Vol. II.

About that time John appears to have run out of ready cash with which to fee his gaoler, so he wrote to the Queen, asking for her assistance. His undated letter[31], (which was probably written in May), is reproduced and transcribed below.

> To the Queenes most Excellent Ma.tie
>
> The humble petition of John Southworth
> prisoner in the Gatehouse
>
> Sheweth
>
> That the pet.r having visited some sick of the plague; as hee hath daily don, since the plague begun; and releeved them and others, ready to starve and perish with almes, given by yo.r Ma.tie and other charitable people. In the latter end of this labor: Mr. White, Curate of Westminster, cominge neere unto the place, where the pet.r was, and seing him come out of an infected house: was much offended therewith: complayned of him; and soe farre prevayled: that S.r Dudley Carlton Clerk to his Ma.ties privie Councell, directed a warrant to the Keeper of the Gatehouse, commanded him to take the pet.r into his charge, and deteyn him in prison, w.ch hee hath don ever since.
>
> May it therefore please yo.r Excellencie, to move his Ma.tie that (seing the pet.r laboreth, only to preserve the poore from perishing; w.ch hee thought wold neither offend his Ma.tie nor the State) it wold graciously please his Ma.tie to give the pet.r leave, to goe to his frends, for meanes; that hee himselfe may not nowe perish in prison.
>
> And the pet.r will (as in duty bound) ever pray for both yo.r Ma.ties.
>
> Southworth

---

[31] *MS. Clarendon State Papers* 13, item 1033. Reproduced by kind permission of the Bodleian Library, Oxford.

To the Queene's most Excellent Matie: [Majesty]

The humble petition of John Southworth
prisoner in the Gatehouse

Sheweth

That the petr [petitioner] having visited some sick of the plague: as hee hath daily don, since the plague begun: and releeved them and others, ready to starve and perish wth almes, given by yor Matie, and other charitable people. In the latter end of this labor: Mr. White, curate of Westminster, coming neare unto the place, wheare the petr was, and seing him come out of an infected house: was much offended therewth: complained of him: and so farre prevayled: that Sr Dudley Carlton, Cleark to his Maties privie Councell, directed a warrant to the Keeper of the Gatehouse, commanded him to take the petr into his chardg, and deteyn him in prison, wch he hath don ever since.

May it therefore please yor Excellencie to move his Matie that seing the petr labored, only to preserve the poore from perishing (wch hee thought wold neither offend his Matie nor the State) it wold gratiously please his Matie to give the petr leave to goe to his frends for meanes: that hee himself may not nowe perish in prison.

And the petr will (as in duty bound) ever
pray for both Yor Maties,

Southworth.

There was a positive response and, according to Prynne, the Queen and Sir Francis Windebank, (the Secretary of State), managed to have John released and *'his finall triall put off, to the great discontent of the people…neere the very time that Dr. Bastwick, Mr. Burton and Mr. Prynne were most grievously censured in the Star Chamber [and] most barbarously pillory'd, deprived of their ears, stigmatized*[32].' This sentence against the three Puritans was carried out in June 1637 and by that time the plague was abating[33].

In that same month John contributed a further £50 to the Seculars and in November he is known to have been temporarily imprisoned, with *'no serious restraint,'* to get him out of the clutches of a priest-catcher. (As they were only paid when, or if, a priest was convicted, priest-catchers had adopted a more lucrative strategy – demanding cash in return for immediate release – when another catcher would watch for an opportunity to arrest him: Whitfield).

Little is recorded about Saint John during the following decade, but presumably he continued his daily round – ministering to those in the London/Westminster slums and collecting monies for the local poor and for prisoners who could not afford to buy privileges from the warders. Perhaps there was also intermittent contact with his family.

One thing, however, is certain. John was working against a background of civil upheaval – the great struggles between the King and Cromwell, which were wracking the British Isles – and he would see/hear at least some of it at first hand.

---

[32] Some of Prynne's prolific leaflets brought him serious trouble and this particular punishment was for a supposed libel against the Royal family.
[33] Purdie, quoting Besant's *London in the Time of the Stuarts'*. Major outbreaks occurred in 1603 (30,361 deaths), 1625 (35,417 deaths), 1636 when 12,102 died and the Great Plague in 1665, which killed 68,596. In addition there were approx. 1,000 – 4,000 deaths annually, because plague was seldom absent.

CHAPTER II

POLITICAL AND RELIGIOUS BATTLES: 1638-1653

THE CHURCH OF ENGLAND

The Anglican Episcopal system which had superceded the Monastic Age, was a middle course between Roman Catholicism and Genevan Calvanism. As a committed Anglican, with firm beliefs and a strong conscience, King Charles was beset by the respective agendas of the Papacy and the Presbyterians, who were each determined to impose their form of church government on Britain. In addition, they objected to Bishops of the Established Church sitting in the House of Lords, where, as part of the government they were also influential in civil affairs.

Charles, a man of great principle and conviction, believed implicitly in the divine right of anointed kings[34] and resolved to strengthen the Church of England and unite his kingdoms under the one Church with the Crown over all, but Cromwell[35] and his associates were bent on the destruction of the Church of England and in particular, the practices which they considered, reflected Roman influence.

TROUBLES IN THE KINGDOM OF SCOTLAND

It was even worse in Scotland, where the King's plan stirred up a hornets' nest. The evangelical Presbyterians considered Bishops in government to be 'popish' and believed that the prescribed form of Service was a first step towards returning the

---

[34] *White King*: Leanda de Lisle. Also King James, who published a book on Kingship & statecraft for Charles' elder brother, Henry, in 1598; (Ed. Jas. Craigie). An extract from *The Basilikon Doron* is on p.101.
[35] Unless otherwise stated, all Information about Cromwell is taken from *The Writings & Speeches of Oliver Cromwell, Vols. I, II & III*, (Ed. by W.C. Abbott), and *Civil War* by Trevor Royle.

country to Roman Catholicism – it would limit their extemporaneous worship and destroy the Kirk.

The Scots framed a National Covenant in February 1638, to which Charles was expected to submit – and their loyalty would be conditional on his defending the right of the people to worship in their own way. (Royle). It was illegal, possibly treasonous and the King was exasperated.

The dead-line for liturgical change was Easter and Archbishop Laud, (who was anti-Puritan), by-passed the Scottish Primate to implement the Scottish Prayer Book. It caused widespread antagonism and rioting – the Covenanters purchased arms from the Low Countries, introduced military training and reversed Laud's policies. They abolished Bishops and Prayer Books, and returned the Kirk to the jurisdiction of Presbytery, Synod and General Assembly. *"Episcopacy,"* the Covenanters said, *"was both un-constitutional and against God's law."*

King and Covenanters were on a collision course – if Bishops were illegal in Scotland, they would be in England. The Covenanters were urged to exclude England from the resolution, but the Scots were adamant – everyone had to become Presbyterians.

The King was advised to send an armed force to restore law and order and Bishop William Juxton, (the Treasurer), allocated £200,000 for the purpose – but they encountered a problem – Elizabeth's remarkable reign had bequeathed many subsequent years of peace – the militia was no longer battle-ready and the idea of fighting their fellow countrymen was abhorrent.

THE FIRST BISHOPS' WAR: 1639.

Charles however, gained the advantage in the first campaign, (in North-East Scotland) and compromised – Scottish ecclesiastical matters could be governed by Assemblies and civil matters by

Parliament. But it was not enough for the Scots. After approaching France and the Puritan-dominated Commons for support, they re-mustered in January 1640, determined to invade England.

The King re-convened the English Parliament in April and Cromwell returned as MP for Cambridge, becoming a multiple *'committeeman'*. Charles appealed for funds *'to punish the Scots and preserve the realm'*, but the Commons had grievances and were determined that he would listen to them first – in addition to the growth of Roman Catholic influence, they objected to the King's personal rule and tax-raising powers; a more democratic form of government was expected before they allocated funds. (This 'Long' Parliament included eighteen of Cromwell's relatives and by the time it ended there were many more, plus those who later married into his family).

During that summer, John Southworth was hauled up before the *'Commissioners of Causes Ecclesiastic,'* where he was described as a *'popish recusant'*. He refused to give sufficient bond to re-appear and *'answer the matters objected against him'*, so was bundled back in the *Clink*. Once again Sir Francis came to John's aid and, *'within few days after he was absolutely released by secretary Windebank's Warrant'*, which reads:-

'THese are to will and require you forthwith on the sight hereof, to enlarge and set at liberty the body of John Southworth *lately committed to your custody. For which this shall be your Warrant. Dated at my house in* Drury-lane, *16th July,* 1640.

Fran. Windebank.'

THE SECOND BISHOPS' WAR: 1640.

The Covenanters invaded England on 17th August – determined *'to protect Scotland's religion,'* help the English puritans *'throw off episcopal rule'* and impose Presbyterianism. As Charles had insufficient funds to keep a standing army, and the 'grassroots' English are a peace-loving people, he once again had recruiting problems. The Royalists lost Northumberland and the Scots' occupation lasted for twelve months. They humiliated the King – the more concessions he made, the more they demanded.

The Commons met in November to dismantle the Tudor system of government, resolve the Scottish crisis, (for which the English Exchequer eventually paid £300,000), and take action against the King's advisors. Amongst these were the Lord Lieutenant of Ireland Earl of Strafford, Archbishop Laud and Sir Francis Windebank. The latter had freed about twenty-seven priests/Jesuits, halted proceedings against seventy-four others and was believed to correspond with the Papal agent, (Whitfield), but he managed to obtain a passport from the King and escape to France.

Strafford and Laud were later executed by Bill of Attainder, (which allowed 'traitors' to be put to death *'without recourse to law'),* and from his cell window in the Tower, the Archbishop managed to bless the Earl as he went to the block.

POWER STRUGGLES

In the Spring of 1641, some of the Puritans were still complaining to the King about *'the great increase of Popery and employing of Popish recusants…in places of power and trust…'* Eventually, in the autumn Windebank's successor, Sir Edward Nicholas, wrote twice to Charles, stating that *'popery (which is generally exceeding distasteful to your subjects of this kingdom) is too much favoured by your clergy here, and in your own court, and that this opinion hath and doth (more than anything) prejudice your Majesty in the esteem and affection of your people.'*

Charles set out for Scotland on 10th August, intending to make peace with the Covenanters and seek re-assurance of support from his Scottish aristocracy. Pym and his party were opposed to the move, because they would not be able to keep an eye on him, but they turned the situation to their advantage. By introducing a *'Parliamentary Ordinance'* to implement 'laws' and a *'Committee of Defence'*, they bypassed royal authority and gave themselves all but regency status. They were now only a step away from controlling the armed forces and at least some of them desired a republic. Their tax demands made the King's requests seem very modest – there were riots, many turned against them and Charles returned from Scotland, *'more popular than when he went away.'*

In September Cromwell spoke in Parliament against the Book of Common Prayer[36] and, without either the consent of the King or the assent of the Lords, he and his colleagues sidelined the Episcopalians and agreed to remove the *'last rags of Rome'* from the Anglican Church:- Diocese, Bishops and Deans; parishes, priests and rectors; Church Courts, Bishops in the House of Lords, and the levying of tithes to support the Established Church. In addition, they took exception to Roman vestments, saints' days, Church Festivals, a set liturgy, the sign of the Cross at baptism, the ring in the marriage ceremony and games/sports profaning the Lord's Day. They wanted to choose their own

---

[36] Presumably the 1604 edition.

ministers, meet, read and interpret Scripture for themselves, invite extemporary prayers, prophesyings/outpourings of the Holy Spirit by individuals, and set up 'lectureships' to supplement Services.

Cromwell played a leading part in framing the ordinance to remove *'popish fittings'* from Anglican churches:- Crucifixes and Rood Screens, Altars and Communion Rails, stained glass windows and idolatrous images, together with *'scandalous pictures'* of the Trinity and Virgin Mary. The House also ordered Communion Tables to be moved from the east end of the churches, candlesticks, tapers and basins taken off them and *'all corporal bowing at the name of Jesus, or towards the east end of the church,'* dispensed with. Sermons were permitted on Sunday afternoons but dancing etc. was forbidden. Their actions drew the line between Non-Conformists and Anglicans and in time this was identified as *'the commencement of civil war.'*

TROUBLES IN THE KINGDOM OF IRELAND

Suddenly the King's problems increased – without warning, Ulster erupted on 22nd/23rd October. Whilst in office, the Earl of Strafford Lord Lieutenant of Ireland, had held the country together, but his prejudice against the Irish Catholics and his denial of their rights, had been offensive and contentious. As they captured key planter strongholds, their leader, Sir Phelim O'Neill, forbid butchery but *'some priests [were] urging that it was no sin to kill Protestants, because they were already damned and beyond redemption;'* (Royle). *'...Some thousands of Protestants [were] massacred, [and the] abhorrence and fear of all that Rome stood for, was one of the contributory causes of the [civil] war*[37]*'*. (Reynolds). Hundreds of refugees crossed over to mainland Britain, Parliament again strictly adhered to *'the laws in force against Jesuits, priests and popish*

---

[37] This was the beginning of the *Confederates' War*: 1641-1653.

recusants' and the papal Agent to the Queen left England, after being *'obliged to make it clear'* to Charles that he could expect no help from the Pope, unless he changed his religion.

(Even when Butler was writing his *'Memoirs'* in 1647, there were still three points which, he noted, were causing grave concern to *'the average thoughtful Protestant:'*

> 1st *'That the Pope, or the Church, have power to absolve all persons of what ever quality they may be, from the obedience due to the civil government, established in the kingdom of England.*
> 2nd *That it is lawful in itself, or by the dispensation of the Pope, to violate a promise, or oath, made to a heretic.*
> 3rd *That it is lawful, by the dispensation, or by the commandment, of the Pope, or of the Church, to kill, destroy, or outrage, and offend, in any other manner, any person whatever, or several persons, of what condition soever they be, for this reason, that they are accused, condemned, censured, or excommunicated for error or heresy.'*
> Purdie).

In November, the Queen failed to get the two senior heirs out of the country and parliament delivered another blow – a *'Grand Remonstrance'* aimed at dismantling Royal Absolutism. They dredged up everything possible to discredit Charles, MPs toured the country, encouraging people to *resist* him and the debate on the *'Great Indictment of the Monarchy'*, lasted fourteen hours. *'It was the most bitterly fought and most momentous argument in the history of the English Parliament'* and they nearly came to blows. Although it was eventually carried with a few votes *'by the hour of the night'*, Pym's party was in the minority.

 In January 1642 Charles appeared in the House of Commons to arrest those who had treasonously encouraged the Scots, (a foreign power), to invade

England, but the culprits, including Pym and Cromwell's cousin Hampden, were forewarned by the Queen's treacherous lady-in-waiting and hid in the Court of the King's Bench [38].

When the Commons took control of the City's militia, the Royalists urged Charles to counter-attack, but he was afraid of plunging the city into anarchy. Instead, he stepped back from the situation and took his family to Hampton Court.

Parliament became divided as petitions favouring monarchy and episcopacy poured into the Commons. Many left and the orderly process of government broke down.

Two years of service on various committees had given Cromwell a wide, working knowledge of public business and affairs. By March he was rapidly rising to importance under Pym and Hampden and the vote to raise an army, (ostensibly *'for the safety of the King's person and the defence of both realms'*), was carried. The Earl of Essex was appointed General, the Earl of Warwick was given command of the fleet and, under pretence of re-arming to sort out the Irish problem), Cromwell secretly put about £1,000 into a subscription fund for *'the cause.'*

VANDALISM

Clergy met strong opposition when they tried to impose the Parliamentary edict to demolish every *'Monument of Superstition and Idolatry…all statues, [etc.] which should be found in churches, or on the crosses in churchyards…'* Many local clashes and scuffles broke out and Richard Baxter, (a minister at Kidderminster and *'one of the finest chroniclers of the war'*), had his life threatened and had to leave his parish when he tried to obey the order.

Clergy were jostled, turned out and *'replaced by army chaplains, who demanded offerings for the cause.'* London was in uproar.

---

[38] L. de Lisle.

Parliament's *Nineteen Propositions* to the King, which were pushed through by Pym and Hampden, were a virtual demand for unconditional surrender. Episcopal votes would be abolished and the King's *'evil counsellors'* replaced. He was expected to give up control of the militia, the Tower of London, (which was the State prison), castles and forts, command of the fleet and the right to approve ministers and advisers. In addition, Catholics would be excluded from the House of Lords and existing laws enforced against them; their children would be educated as Protestants by Protestants and the Established Church would become Presbyterian. They also demanded that he distance himself from his wife and give up the care and education of the children. In return for this surrender of sovereignty, he would be given a larger revenue than his forebears.
Charles refused to sign.

'The whole business of the matter', wrote the Earl of Clarendon, *'was whether the King was above Parliament, or Parliament, in ruling, above the King'.* They were poles apart and civil war, with its battles and skirmishes, wars of words, food and fuel shortages, its outbreaks of sickness, disease and other horrors, was inevitable. In February 1642, Charles managed to ship the Queen, their daughter Mary[39], jewels and plate, (for the purchase of munitions), to the Netherlands, but their two youngest children were taken into Parliamentary 'care.'

As the opposing sides recruited and manœuvred for position during the summer, it became horrifyingly clear that very many fathers, sons, brothers, relatives, neighbours and *'dear friends',* would be on opposing sides and fighting each other. (In some cases it must have gone even further, because in the future, Cromwell would discover *'a damsel'* amongst his PoWs.)

---

[39] Charles desperately needed Dutch money, and in 1641 nine year old Mary had been married to the young Prince William of Orange. He reportedly brought £23,000 of gifts with him, as well as a substantial sum in gold. Mary and her governess were due to join Prince William at *The Hague* when she was fourteen years old, but it had become imperative to get her out of England.

THE CIVIL WAR YEARS, 1642-46, 1648-49 and 1649-51.

There was a *'rising tide of Royalism'* and Charles had a good summer. Much of Lancashire was royalist and most Roman Catholics, aristocracy and landed gentry believed in the *'sanctity of majesty'* and declared for the king.

Prince Rupert Count Palatine of the Rhine and his brother, Prince Maurice, travelled to England in August, to support their uncle. They and leading Royalists notched up successes in many parts of the country; morale was high and Charles set up his court, administration centre, Royal Mint and newspaper publishers at Oxford. It became a garrison town and he remained there for three years.

The King gained the advantage in the first pitched battle at Edgehill, Warwickshire (23rd Oct. 1642), the Welsh flocked to join him and Rupert sent in *'a steady stream of prisoners and booty'* throughout autumn and winter.

Iconoclasm, which had been practiced on the continent by Protestants against Roman Catholics, was now being adopted in order to destroy the Anglican church. A further ordinance was issued against the Book of Common Prayer, the wearing of vestments and *'choir singing.'*

After a written warning, in which Cromwell described a *'choir service'* as being *'unedifying and offensive'*, he interrupted a choral service at Ely Cathedral in January 1643. *'…laying his hand on his sword in a passion, [he] bid [the Canon] leave off his fooling and come down; and so drove out the whole congregation'*. At St. Mary's Cambridge, he had the Prayer Book shredded and *'a beautiful carved structure which had not one jot of imagery about it'*, broken up –

the first of the acts of vandalism recorded in churches, but which was replicated all over the country, often by parliamentary armies on the move. (When Peterborough Cathedral was sacked, the fittings were destroyed and the House of God was used to stable their horses).

After Edgehill, a very vocal peace faction developed – petitions and demonstrations against the war became commonplace, but Charles' peace talks, (Feb-Apr), eventually broke down. Pym's party were determined to rule both Church and State, whilst the King was equally determined to protect both.

Parliament's unpopular war taxes and forced loans were increased, many deemed them illegal and refused to pay, but the money had to come from somewhere if the rebels were going to continue the war. Cromwell's solution was simple – the Royalists would have to foot the bill. An ordinance was duly passed, enabling Parliament to sequestrate the estates of *'Delinquents and Papists'*. A fixed scale of payments, known as *'Compounding for Delinquency'* was imposed and fines were generally set at 5% of the delinquent's property, or a year's revenue. The scheme brought in huge sums of money for the rebels.

Parliament raised four federated armies, to be based in the West, North, Midlands and East respectively. They were to defend their counties and raise horse, foot and funds etc. for *'the cause'*. Sir Thomas Fairfax was given command of the Northern Army and Cromwell the Eastern. Some 60,000 to 70,000 men, (plus the Scots), needed paying and the Royalists found themselves impoverished and weakened by sequestration. In addition, the revenues of the King, Queen and Prince Rupert were seized, the Commons provided £30,000 for the Scots, (via the Committee of Goldsmith's Hall), and the City was persuaded to lend them £80,000 to help maintain the armies.

Hampden died of war wounds in June and six months later Pym was also dead.

July was a lucrative month for the King: Henrietta Maria had landed in February, having survived a hazardous return journey.

They had been chased by warships and endured two hours of enemy fire at Bridlington, before eventually reaching York, where she had gained many recruits for Charles. In June, with little sleep and not much food, she had travelled South with 3,000 foot, 50 company of horse and dragoons, 6 pieces of canon, 2 mortars and 150 wagon loads of supplies. They were hunted by enemy cavalry, but fought a *'bloody'* and *'desperate'* battle to gain Burton-upon-Trent, took 400 prisoners, then acquired and sold an excessive amount of plunder.

Now, on the 14th, having avoided capture and impeachment for treason, she entered Oxford with her *'imposing [£100,000] convoy, amidst great rejoicing.'* A fortnight later, Prince Rupert captured Bristol and destroyed the Western Association. He commandeered a £100,000 war chest, eighteen merchant vessels and four Parliamentary warships, (the captains and crews being persuaded to change sides).

 Despite having no intention of introducing the Presbyterian system in England, during September Henry Vane the Younger brokered an agreement with the Scots, ratified their political/religious *'Solemn League and Covenant'* and then led a military executive, the *'Committee of Both Kingdoms'*, to direct the war; (doubtless ignoring complaints about Lancashire Parliamentarians *'still making excursions into Craven [to] get horses, cattle and sheep, from off the lands of those in arms against Parliament'*).

In December 3,000 Irish soldiers, cattle and £20,000, were landed on the Wirral – in return for a twelve-month armistice agreed between King and Confederates and the promise to consider repealing the penal laws, granting freedom of worship and the temporary retention of about 90% of Ireland, which they had captured. Charles appeared to have all the advantages.

January 1644 saw a Scots' army over 20,000-strong crossing the Tweed to support Parliament, (for £30,000 per month) and *'uniformity of religion.'*

Prince Rupert opposed Cromwell at the Battle of Marston Moor, (2nd July) and, although it was a turning point, the outcome was not sufficiently decisive. Charles held intermittent talks with the rebels, but failed to reach agreement and the Queen returned to France, where she headed a small court-in-exile and tried to raise support for the King.

There was perhaps some retaliation going on in the autumn, because the Commons agreed that half the collections taken on the 12th September in London, Westminster, and those churches lying *'within lines of communication,'* would be sent to relieve Lancashire, where Rupert's Royalists had caused *'famine and distress.'*

Parliament also passed an ordinance forbidding quarter to *'any Irishman or Papist born in Ireland',* who was taken prisoner in England. Cromwell considered that hanging Irish soldiers was *"a righteous judgement of God upon these barbarous wretches"* and they were treated outrageously. After giving warning, Rupert retaliated and the practice was discontinued.

During the winter it was confidently noted that *'our noble and active Colonel Cromwell [was] an astute military commander…a brave, decisive soldier in battle'*, but despite their vote of confidence, after two years of civil conflicts and the support of Puritans from New England, Holland, Ireland, Wales and Scotland, Charles was still not beaten.

Cromwell needed a plan.

The answer lay in a well-paid, *'new modelled army'* and, although he was keen to recruit those who believed in *'the cause'*, the majority of his ranks were professionals. (Peaceful occupations had been interrupted by wars at home and abroad and many were driven into the army by financial necessity. English and foreigners alike, enlisted where they could).

Fairfax, (one of the few officers who were not MPs), was appointed Commander-in-Chief. Experience and stern discipline moulded the *new modelled army* and the *'Ironsides'*, (Cavalry), into the most sober, formidable force known; (they had a chaplain and anyone caught swearing was fined a shilling).

It was the beginning of the end for Charles, whose eclectic ranks – Welsh Episcopalians, Scottish Presbyterians, Irish Catholics and English Royalists – were divided by doctrine, geography and distrust of each other.

In January 1645, Archbishop Williams of York, (a distant relative of Cromwell's), warned Charles against him, saying:

'That Cromwell, taken into the Rebel's Army by his Cousin Hampden, was the most dangerous Enemy that His Majesty had. For tho' he were at that time of mean Rank and Use among them, yet he would climb higher. I knew him at Bugden, but never knew his religion. He was a Common Spokesman for Sectaries, and maintain'd their Part with stubbornness. He never discours'd as if he were pleas'd with your Majesty, and your great Officers; and indeed he loves none that are more than his Equals. Your

Majesty did him but justice in repulsing a Petition put up by him against Sir Thomas Steward, of the Isle of Ely; but he takes them all for his Enemies, that would not let him undo his best Friend; and above all that live, I think he is the most mindful of an Injury. He talks openly that it is fit some should act more vigorously against your Forces, and bring your Person into the Power of the Parliament. He cannot give a good Word of his General the Earl of Essex, because he says the Earl is but half an Enemy to your Majesty, and hath done you more Favour than Harm. His Fortunes are broken, that it is impossible for him to subsist, much less to be what he aspires to, but by your Majesty's Bounty, or by the Ruin of us all, and a common Confusion. In short, every Beast hath some evil Properties; but Cromwel hath the Properties of all evil Beasts. My humble Motion is, that either you would win him to you by Promises of fair Treatment, or catch him by some Strategem, and cut him short.'

On 1st February Henry Morse was hanged. (He had returned to England two years previously and been arrested, but the Queen had not been in a position to help). A nearby priest, however, gave Henry absolution, '*according to an agreement between them*' and Purdie suggests that perhaps John Southworth was there for Henry, as he had been for Edmund Arrowsmith.

In effect, by April/May, Cromwell's group were running the country and martial law was in place. When Richard Baxter visited the soldiers after the Battle of Naseby, (14th June), he wrote: – '*I found a new face of things which I never dreamt of: I heard the plotting Heads very hot upon that which intimated their Intention to subvert both Church and State…a few proud, self-conceited, hot-headed Sectaries had got into the highest places, and were Cromwell's chief favourites, and by their very heat and activity, bore down the rest, or carried them along with them, and were the Soul of the Army…though being not one to twenty throughout the Army, I perceived that they took the King for a Tyrant and an Enemy, and really intended absolutely to master him, or to ruine him; and that they thought if they might fight against him, they might kill or conquer him; and if they might conquer, they were never more to trust him further than he was in their power; They said, "What were the Lords of England but William the Conquerour's Colonels? or the Barons but his Majors? or the Knights but his Captains?"*

Baxter recalled that he had been invited to be Pastor of *'that famous Troop which [Cromwell] began his Army with [and that] his Officers purposed to make the Troop a gathered Church…'* He had refused at the time and then regretted it, but was anxious now, because the army was developing a political character and becoming a law unto itself. Charles, meanwhile, privately admitted that the turn of events had reduced him *'from a very prosperous position to so low an ebb as to be a perfect trial of all men's integrities to me.'*

Being very worried, the Catholic Earl of Glamorgan took independent action for Charles, well *'beyond instructions'* and struck a 'secret' deal with the *'Irish Confederates' Supreme Council'* to supply a new army for the King, but the Pope and Kings of France and Spain immediately took an interest and sent their representatives to meet the Council. A very persuasive nuncio, (Papal ambassador), drew big concessions from the gullible Glamorgan, who was led to believe that a re-established Roman Catholic Church in Ireland would lend support to Charles and defeat the New Model Army. But the secret was soon out, Parliament was outraged and concluded that the King must be a closet Catholic, supported by the Counter Reformation. Embarrassed, Charles distanced himself from Glamorgan and revoked the deal.

By the beginning of 1646 the King had lost too much territory; (Lancashire, for example, had no Royalists left in arms). Charles was Sovereign in name only and Parliament was in control. Despite the Scots being the original authors of his misfortunes, in May he took up a previous invitation, travelled to Newark and put himself under their protection. The Scots, realising that they would never attain Presbyterian Church government under Cromwell, seized this new opportunity. Charles was effectively their prisoner – they refused him Anglican rites and tried to brainwash and bully him into adopting Presbyterianism.

The next month Charles ordered all his forces to disband and the sequestrators promptly targeted the lesser gentry and yeomen, (which explains why at least five Samlesbury tenants were fined for *delinquency*).

Back in Ireland the Pope's nuncio mounted a coup at the end of August, took command of the *Supreme Council* and made it clear that his objective was the re-establishment of the Catholic Church in Ireland and the restoration of the Irish branch of his family to their lands in Scotland. He was certainly not going to help the King regain his throne[40].

At this time the Presbyterians had the upper hand in Parliament, Presbyterian church government was introduced and ministers were supported by sequestration funds. The French agent in London however, recorded that *'the credit of the Independents increases every day'* and the *'opportune'* and *'mysterious'* death of the Earl of Essex, (one of their chief opponents), gave rise to suspicions that he had been poisoned.

By now, Cromwell was serving on several of the committees which were running the country, including the *Committee of Both Kingdoms* – which was supposedly subordinate to both Parliaments. (The Speakers of the Houses were custodians of

---

[40] The nuncio stayed until Feb. 1649, when, infuriated by the squabbles and intrigues of the Irish (and perhaps knowing of Cromwell's planned invasion), he excommunicated his opposition and left Ireland.

the *Mace* and Reynolds notes that no priests were executed[41] between 1646 and May 1651 – presumably because Cromwell and his colleagues were concentrating on their rebellion).

Cromwell signed over the £400,000 owed by *'the Kingdom of England to the Kingdom of Scotland, for the assistance to the said Kingdom by virtue of the treaties between the two Kingdoms of 29th November 1643'*. Repayments totalling £50,000 were also due to various individuals and the English Royalists accused the Scots of having *'sold their King.'*

December's negotiations between Charles and the rebels were fruitless; the Royalists believed that the negotiators had no intention of reaching an agreement with Charles, whilst the rebels blamed the King – he was refusing to agree to their *'reasonable proposals.'*

On 1st February 1647 the Scots' army left England. Charles was transferred into the 'care' of the English commissioners at Holdenby House, Northamptonshire, where he received better treatment, but was still denied Anglican rites.

Cromwell was strongly criticised during the spring, suffered from *'a dangerous impostume in the head'*, kept a low profile and avoided Parliament, which left his Independents *'weaker in the House.'* (It was probably connected with Commons' discussions in January, about augmenting Cromwell's income with land *'confiscated from papists and delinquents and not yet disposed of'*).

There was growing dissatisfaction in the army, as Parliament decided to disband the force and send some of them to Ireland without paying arrears – but they were now professional veterans, they had helped to bring in a new order and were bitter. The *agitators,* (ie. shop stewards), who protected their interests in the Commons, were new men of lower social status

---

[41] From Lingard Vol. VIII: There was one execution in May 1651, but afterwards the ascendant Independents – who claimed they were the champions of religious liberty – *'shrunk from the odium of such sanguinary exhibitions and transported the rest of the prisoners to the continent'*.

and radical opinions – men with personal ambitions and grievances who had risen through the ranks. Most disliked the King and wanted a new parliament which could rule without consent from the Sovereign or assent from the Lords. They wanted exemption from future impressment, pensions for their widows and orphans, and suffrage, *'a right to the kingdom [for] all the freeborn'*, which would allow them to take their place in national affairs alongside property owners.

By May, many Agitators had filled the empty seats in the Commons and a *'Council of Army Officers'* was formed as an Upper House, to stand against the authority of Parliament. It was a dangerous development. Ireton and Cromwell emerged as the dominant members of the new council and if Fairfax was ill, it was Cromwell who presided.

Charles, meanwhile, was trying to negotiate a deal with anyone and everyone – Parliament, the City, the army, Royalists in all three Kingdoms, Presbyterians, Independents, Scots and French. When he drew close to an agreement with the Presbyterians, Cromwell became worried, knowing that if that happened, the Scots would unite with them and he and his Independents would be doomed. Consequently, on 3rd June Cornet Joyce, *(a radical firebrand)*, was given five hundred troopers and sent to seize the sovereign. Charles was then placed under house arrest at Childerley Hall, near Cambridge.

Reasoning that they could subdue the army once they had Cromwell in the Tower, the moderate MPs planned to seize him the following day in the House of Commons; but Cromwell found out, fled and took refuge with the army, (despite having previously assured Parliament that he had entirely disassociated himself from them).

Sir William Waller, (Presbyterian), wrote that Cromwell had claimed to know nothing of the army's *'mutinous proceedings [and] invoked the curse of God upon himself and his posterity if ever he should join or combine with them in any actings or attempts contrary to the orders of the House'*. Meantime, the Levellers were accusing him of treachery to the army, and Lilburne wrote that he did not go to them, *'until the danger of imprisonment forced him to fly to the army.'*

On arrival, Cromwell found a very agitated Fairfax agonising over Joyce's abduction of the King and demanding of Henry Ireton, (Cromwell's son-in-law), *"who gave those orders?"* Ireton tried to deflect the blame, but Joyce, (who eventually had to carry the responsibility), asserted that he had obeyed Lieutenant-General Cromwell's orders exactly. According to Clarendon, the Presbyterians knew that it would not have been done without the Lieutenant-General's *'direction'* and he wrote:-

'Cromwell had the ascendant over him [General Fairfax], purely by his dissimulation and pretence of conscience and sincerity. There is no doubt Fayrefax did not then, nor long after, believe that the other, [Cromwell], had those wicked designs in his heart against the King, or the least imagination of disobeying the Parliament…'

 In July, Lambert and Ireton drew up a new Constitution for England – a compromise which included:

- The restoration of the Royal family;
- Biennial sessions for Parliament;
- A Council of State to replace the Privy Council;

- The abolition of Bishops, but no imposition of the Covenant;
- A militia under Parliamentary control for ten years.

The City was hit by riots: Londoners were dismayed at having to pay the cost of a standing army[42] and most recognized that the King's proposals – the giving up of episcopacy for three years and control of the militia for ten – were the most reasonable and they demanded a return to normality and a brokered peace.

On the 26th some of the mob held the Speaker in his chair, whilst others forced the remaining members of the Commons to pass a resolution to recall the King on the terms he had suggested in May, but Fairfax brought soldiers into the City to restore order.

Charles followed events with great interest and when the apprentices signed a petition for his restoration, he rejected Ireton and Lambert's solution.

1647 was probably the most controversial time of Cromwell's life. Accusations and questions regarding double dealing, kingnapping and hypocrisy, were rife:-

- Was he pretending to uphold Parliamentary sovereignty, whilst encouraging the Agitators secretly and denouncing them publicly – sowing dissension and setting Parliament and army against each other, then using the said army to rise higher?
- Did he order the capture of the King?
- Did he set the Presbyterians and Independents against each other?

(Two phrases in the Archbishop of York's written warning to Charles, however, may also be worth noting:-

---

[42] Royle: Twelve months later, the army was costing the government £100,000 per month.

'...indeed he loves none that are more than his Equals' [and] 'above all that live, I think he is the most mindful of an Injury').

Abbott acknowledges that, whilst Cromwell <u>did</u> attend the House of Commons, <u>did</u> protest his allegiance to Parliament, (with tears and great emotion), <u>did</u> maintain relations with the army, (despite protesting that he had severed his links with them), <u>did</u> leave Parliament more or less secretly to take refuge with the army, before becoming a member of their council and dominating it – he did not plot the end from the beginning. Rather, he took advantage of opportunities as they arose and changed with the constantly fluctuating circumstances – had he not done so, he would have found himself in the Tower, or worse. His silences deceived more than his words.

In August, it was Cromwell who led the cavalry through London in a massive demonstration of military strength, even though he was still (supposedly) subordinate to the commander-in-chief, Sir Thomas Fairfax. Fairfax had been ill, and was relegated to a carriage behind, with Lady Fairfax and Mrs. Cromwell. The City was cowed, Parliament surrendered and the capital was put under military control. It was another step towards absolute power – Fairfax was made Constable of the Tower and became little more than a figure-head, later claiming that they *"set my name...to all their papers, whether I consented or not."*

Cromwell realised that they could soon be facing a new alliance of King, Scots, the City and Presbyterians. He was particularly critical of two parliamentary Presbyterians, saying, *"I know nothing to the contrary, but that I am as well able to govern the country as either of them",* and moved quickly – apparently intent on finding some *'middle ground'* with the King and doing a deal for his Independents. The King, (now at Hampton Court), also had frequent visits from Presbyterian Fairfax.

Autumn was critical: Cromwell was debating and voting in Parliament, whilst keeping his options open with the King's representatives and Charles was using the negotiations as a means of buying time for the Hamiltons to finalize arrangements in Scotland.

Elsewhere, it was noticed that Ireton, (who Lilburne referred to as *'the cunningest of Machivellians'*), had a *'stubbornness towards the King and [it was feared], that he often prevailed upon Cromwell against his own inclinations, [that] the King's person was in danger and there was some secret design on his life.'* Again there were suspicious questions – if Charles was eliminated, what then? Was Cromwell planning to make himself *'master of the state',* and take the place of their crowned and anointed king? Their fears of treachery were well-founded and Cromwell *'scarce had a friend left in the House.'*

The English felt like a conquered nation at the mercy of their conquerors. They bitterly resented military occupation and disturbances continued around the country; but the Royalists were stymied – their king was imprisoned, their ranks decimated by the first civil war and their experienced leaders either dead, or in exile. They themselves had been disarmed and their strongholds destroyed or dismantled, they were impoverished by sequestration/compounding and spied on by both official and unofficial intelligence agents.

IMPASSE

There was deep distrust on both sides and an impasse was rapidly approaching:-

- The King was determined to guard episcopacy and be restored with as few conditions as possible;
- The Presbyterians were still determined to fully implement their system of church government;

- The Independents, who controlled the army and considered themselves Republicans, were bent on religious tolerance sans Episcopalian or Presbyterian interference;

- The Scots were lurking over the Border, ready to support the King;

- The army and Parliament were each trying to get the King on board, whilst the Agitators and Levellers, (now increasing in both numbers and influence), were convinced that Cromwell and Ireton had come to some secret agreement with the King. They proposed to abolish King, Lords and Established Church and use the dissension to induce anarchy;

- Fairfax was determined to get the army paid. Discipline was declining as they waited for justice and he suggested that church lands could be sold to pay arrears;

- Parliament insisted on being the dominant power in the State and refused to disband the army;

- As if that was not enough, there was discontent in the fleet and the Irish problem was still simmering.

The quick fix that Cromwell needed, was as far off as ever. He was at odds with Parliament and desperate to legalize his position. With the City hostile, a Scottish invasion would be disastrous for him.

In November, Charles was warned that some fanatical Leveller guards were planning to murder him and he escaped on the night of the 12th. Bungled arrangements, however, meant he was soon recaptured and imprisoned in Carisbrooke Castle, under the watchful eye of another of Cromwell's relatives.

On the 16th Charles added further concessions – he would also agree to:-

- bishops being assisted by presbyters, both in jurisdiction and ordination;
- eventual full liberty of worship to all except Roman Catholics and atheists;
- surrender of his control of the militia for the rest of his life.

The nation was war-weary and agreement possible, but everyone was suspicious of everyone else. When the Scots formally protested about the Independents' ill-treatment of Charles, the Independents realized that agreement had been reached and countered it with further exacting proposals.

Berkeley, the King's messenger, became deeply disturbed when a Parliamentary General-Officer, (who spied for Charles), told him to tell the King, *"...that we, since the tumults of the Army, did mistrust* Cromwell *and, not long after,* Ireton *; whereof I informed you. I come now to tell you, that we mistrust neither; but know them, and all of us, to be the archest villains in the world. For we, [the Council of Officers], are resolved, notwithstanding our engagements, to destroy the King and his Posterity ; to which* Ireton *made two Propositions, this afternoon ; one, that you [the King] should be sent prisoner to* London, *the other, that none should speak with you upon pain of death…and then bring [you] to trial ; and I dare think no farther. This will be done in ten days ; and therefore, if the King can escape, let him do it as he loves his life*[43].*"*

Berkeley continues, *'I then inquired what was the reason of this horrid change; what had the King done to deserve it ; He said, "Nothing ; and that to our grief ; for, we would leap for joy, if we could have any advantage against him. I have pleaded hard against this Resolution this day ; but have been laughed at for my pains."*

---
[43] There are believed to have been two attempts, but neither was successful.

Berkeley then asked him what he thought had brought all this about. The spy was not sure, but thought that, because the army was not sufficiently *'quelled'*, there may be schism and the majority would side with the Presbyterians. He concluded that, *'if we cannot bring the Army to our sense, we must go to theirs.'*

'And therefore,' continues Berkeley, *'Cromwell bent all his thoughts to make his peace with the Party that was most opposite to the King…'*

So the Royalists finally realized that the King's enemies wanted his death, not his abdication. Support for Charles and opposition to Parliament increased, whilst the Independents, (principally Cromwell and Ireton), knew that they would pay for it with their lives if the King was restored. The Levellers were as much opposed to the ascendancy of Cromwell as to monarchy, and Marten, (a prominent party member), was reported to be so convinced of Cromwell's treachery, that he had taken to carrying both a dagger and a pistol, in order to *'despatch'* him, should he abandon them.

On 24th December, there was a *'great prayer-meeting'* of the Council of Officers, opened by Cromwell, Ireton *'and others'*. After much prayer and Scripture reading, a resolution *'to destroy the King and his Posterity'* was confirmed in *'great secrecy.'*

As the Independents pushed for a purge of Parliament, the Presbyterians started to *'melt away'* and the army obtained its majority.

In an attempt to discourage possible meetings, Christmas 1647 was 'cancelled', causing further unrest in various places and more demands to restore the King. Shops were ordered to remain open, whilst soldiers patrolled London, pulling down street decorations and checking that no celebratory food was being cooked. Even so, some congregations were defiant – they used the Prayer Book and decorated their churches lavishly with greenery.

The spy's information proved correct – on the 3rd January 1648 two resolutions were adopted:

(i) Anyone contacting the King would be guilty of high treason and no messages were to be received from him; (ii) *'...the King should be prosecuted for his life, as a criminal person...'*

On the same day they also dissolved the *'Committee of Both Kingdoms'*, (thus side-lining the Scots), and then revived it as the *'Committee of Safety/Derby House'* – a supreme executive controlled by Independents and Levellers. Cromwell was the dominant figure and they declared themselves independent of Parliament. Time was spent with various groups, trying to formulate a new system of government, but the discussions were ineffectual – there was discontent throughout the country and most people still preferred the King's proposals.

By the 14th the Independents had, *'by strategy,'* cleared the Commons of Presbyterians. They invited the army to come to Whitehall and by 8.00.am. on the 15th they had seized London.

In February, a ludicrous *'Declaration'* was launched against Charles and the Duke of Buckingham, reviving an earlier charge about conspiring to poison the late King James. It was vigorously supported by Cromwell, but considered *'monstrous and incredible'* by most, and raised violent objections from leading lawyers in the House. After failing to have one of them expelled, Cromwell turned his invective on the institution of monarchical government.

When the question of Cromwell's income came up for discussion again, he was allocated land and property that he valued at £1,680 p.a., but which others claimed was worth £5,000 to £6,000. It antagonized the Levellers still further, but many of them, particularly successful generals, profited greatly from the rewards of confiscated lands allotted to them by Parliament. Others made their fortunes by speculation – buying Royalist estates at a fraction of their value and then selling them on. It was noticed that the Levellers and Republicans, (including Marten), were some of the worst offenders and it added material grievances to the political and spiritual ones of the Royalists.

On 29th April the House voted to retain the fundamental government by King, Lords and Commons, but it was soon over-turned by the army's Council of Officers, who resolved *'that neither this King nor any of his posterity should ever reign Kings of England'*. This, the Royalists felt, justified their claim that the real issue was the supremacy of the military.

For nearly two years there had been no fighting, but Anglican, Presbyterian and Independent elements were still unreconciled and hostility to the military government was breaking out:-

- A petition, (supported by the clergy and signed by 20,000 people), was delivered from Kent, urging a settlement between King and Parliament, the disbandment of the army, a return to government by the old established laws, and the reform of taxation. They occupied the City overnight and when Cromwell sent in the cavalry to quell the demonstrators, some were killed.

- The City was hostile and a new burst of pamphleteering voiced firm loyalty to the King.

- Most counties from Northumberland to Kent were on the verge of insurrection;

- There was mutiny in Wales;

- Various factions in Ireland were planning to unify against the New Model Army;

- The Scots who had engaged to support the King, were making preparations. They had endeavoured to get the Parliamentary fleet to change sides, but were stymied when Vice-Admiral Sir William Batten was demoted and replaced by the Levellers' leader, Colonel Rainsborough. A seed, however, had been sown and in spring the navy put Rainsborough ashore and Batten took eleven warships to Holland to join the Prince of Wales. Six ships in The Downs also mutinied, declared for the King and blocked up Dover.

In July Batten was back – with nineteen ships and eighteen-year-old Prince Charles, all keen to engage with the Lord High Admiral, the Earl of Warwick.

If everyone had been ready at the same time, the uprisings may well have successfully freed England from the grip of the Independents and their New Model Army. Even so, Fairfax, Cromwell and Ireton were fully stretched subduing them all.

THE SECOND CIVIL WAR: THE BATTLE OF RIBBLETON MOOR, PRESTON

After suppressing South Wales and disposing of his prisoners, (two shot and 240 dispatched to Barbados @ 12d. each), Cromwell hurried north to assist Major-General Lambert, who was having trouble with the Engagers heading south, under the Duke of Hamilton. Having reached Yorkshire, Cromwell was informed that the Royalists, under Sir Marmaduke Langdale – had opened the road for the Scots by taking Berwick and Carlisle – and would rendezvous with Hamilton at Preston. Knowing that he had to win, and win decisively, he hurried west.

Unknown to Langdale, (who had travelled south via Settle), Cromwell used the same route between Gisburn and Ribbleton, but the New Model Army camped at Stonyhurst, (16th August), before continuing through Longridge and Grimsargh, (where the Royalists had spent the night).

The weather was atrocious – the summer of 1648 being the worst in living memory. Minor roads were little more than cart-tracks and quickly became quagmires. Progress was a struggle for horse and foot on both sides and wagons sank axle deep. One Scots officer observed later, *'that there were such deluges of rain…that every brook was a river…'*

Langdale, having finally become aware of Cromwell's proximity, sent a warning to Hamilton and left a small cavalry screen near Gamull Lane. In the late afternoon of the 17th, Cromwell found the main Royalist army *'very formidably'* drawn up on Ribbleton Moor in a defile *'very deep and ill, up to the enemy's Army…'*

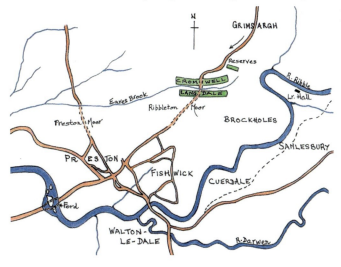

Langdale had deployed his men at the top of the bluff on the Preston side of Eaves Brook, where the Longridge road crosses the stream at Slack Brow. Musketeers were lining the high hedges of the numerous small fields and the pikemen were positioned behind them with their 18 ft. pikes.

The Scots were absent – some were still at Kirkby Lonsdale, some were strung out between Preston Moor and Walton-le-Dale and the cavalry was foraging between Wigan and the Fylde.

So instead of meeting an army of 20,000-plus, Cromwell faced only 3,600.

Although neither muskets nor cavalry could operate efficiently in the driving rain and the mud was much deeper at the bottom of the defile, Cromwell knew an advantage when he saw it. As he later reported, '...*we resolved that night to engage them if we could...*' and, with 8,500 men and only a few hours of daylight left, he attacked – before, Captain Hodgson complained, many of his men *'had come up.'*

Hamilton appeared with *'a few'* Scots lancers and drove back the Parliamentarian horse, who were charging straight down the lane towards Preston. Then Cromwell noted that the Royalists were lessening their defence on the north side of Slack Brow, whilst putting up a *'very stiff and sturdy resistance'* to the south of it. At the same time, Langdale was *'shogging*[44] *down towards the [Walton-le-Dale] Bridge...keeping almost all in reserve, that so he might bring fresh hands often to fight...'* When the Parliamentarians failed to overpower them, Cromwell called up the two regiments of Colonel Ashton's Lancastrian reserves and they tipped the balance.

Previously, the rules of engagement had been observed, but this time the fighting was savage. The Cromwellians, under the impression that they had subdued the country, were wrong – they were mad, they took revenge and no quarter was given. There were *'many men slain, many prisoners taken...'* and Langdale's army was almost totally destroyed. A large mound and boulder in Brockholes are believed to mark the mass grave of some of those killed during this stage of the Preston fight.

---

[44] Moving intermittently by pulses.

Many combatants must have fled across the swollen Ribble into Samlesbury, because nearly three hundred years later, young Samlesbury boys, (unaware that the Preston fight had been of more consequence than any other in the civil wars), gleefully collected bucketsful of musket balls from the riverside fields, to load into their catapults. They were also found on Lower Hall land and local historian, Robert Eaton, recorded in 1936 that several men were killed in a skirmish said to have taken place in *'the pleasant leafy dingle',* near Bezza Brook.

Musket balls were found there too, and superstitious people avoided the adjacent Dean Lane in the dark, in case they encountered the headless horseman! (Side by side, lane and brook border land at the Lower Hall, the traditional birthplace of Saint John Southworth).

Cromwell, (for whom Preston was his first independent command and a famous victory), reported that *'we have many prisoners, and many of those of quality, and many slain and the Army so dissipated*[45]*'.* For Langdale and the inexperienced Hamilton it was a disaster, but Langdale was at least able to record that he kept his post with *'various success, many times gaining ground of the Enemy: and as the Scots acknowledge, they never saw any Foot fight better than mine did'.* But the King lamented that the Preston defeat *"was the worst news that ever came to England."*

Prince Charles had patrolled along the east coast and up the Thames as far as the Medway, but apart from a few minor raids, when they *'took some prizes and issued a proclomation'* and manœuvred with the Parliamentary fleet off Shoeburyness, they achieved little. At the end of August, when a storm blew the opponents apart and drinking water was

---

[45] The battle continued south of Preston and Cromwell later estimated that over-all they had taken 4,000 prisoners, killed 1,000 of the allies, and recovered 4,000 to 5,000 weapons.

becoming scarce, it was decided to return Prince Charles to Holland.

By September, Cromwell had proved that, under his command there was no force in the British Isles which could withstand the New Model Army. He had restored Berwick and Carlisle to England, whilst Scotland had surrendered, (for the time being). The army was now the dominant influence and Cromwell the dominant figure within the army.

Sir Winston Churchill's summary was typically succint:-

'King, Lords and Commons, landlords and merchants, the City and the countryside, Bishops and Presbyters, the Scottish Army, the Welsh people and the English fleet, all now turned against the New Model Army. The Army beat the lot.'

Parliament was almost in abeyance – by September there was only an average of nine Peers and little more than a hundred Commons in their seats, but despite strong opposition from the Levellers and Republicans, the Presbyterians and moderate Independents took advantage of Cromwell's absence in the north to try to settle the issue in a new round of negotiations with the King.

He readily made a number of concessions, (which would erode his position), but again baulked at the abolition of the Book of Common Prayer and Episcopacy being replaced by Presbyterian church government. All sides seem to have totally underestimated the strength of his convictions.

Save for the advanced Independents, most people wanted a *'safe, well-grounded peace'* and inclined to a *'King and Parliament'* government. The Lords accepted the King's plans for a moderate episcopacy and toleration, and were prepared to conclude a treaty – but they needed to get it past Cromwell, who now had many relatives and friends in key positions.

The King's life was in the balance.

A small party of Royalists seized Rainsborough at Doncaster, hoping to exchange him for the imprisoned Langdale, but in the ensuing struggle he was inadvertently killed. The Cromwellians construed it as deliberate murder and his death deepened their hatred towards Charles.

Cromwell, who talked so much about liberty of the individual, approved the sale of *'2,000 common [Scots] prisoners'* to the King of Spain. Although this particular deal fell through when the promised cash failed to materialize, the future would see the Irish prisoners sold in this ruthless, unchristian manner. Cromwell also complained bitterly to the *'Committee for Compounding'*, that the sentences imposed on the Royalists were far too lenient – they had committed *'the unpardonable sin'* of trying to overthrow the army and had come close to succeeding.

By this time most of the old colonels and generals had retired. They had been replaced by men of lower social status and radical opinions, who were ready to go to extremes from which Fairfax and other officers were drawing back – alarmed, dismayed and horrified by developments.

It was inconceivable now, that the King could ever be acquitted, given his freedom and allowed to rule. The rebels had become even more scared for their own safety, so Ireton also demanded the deaths of those who had assisted Charles.

Their situation was discussed at a meeting of Levellers and advanced Independents (15th Nov.) when, John Lilburne said, *"the Independents plainly told us, the chief things first to be done by the Army was first to cut off the King's Head, etc. and force and thoroughly purge, if not dissolve, the Parliament"*. Lilburne had replied that *"It was to the advantage of the people to keep both King and Parliament, however bad they were, as 'one Tyrant to balance another'...and not suffer the Army...to devolve all the government of the Kingdom into their wills and swords...And if we should do this, our slavery for the future...might probably be greater than it ever was…and so our last error would be greater than our first."*

Charles had also realized that the net was closing in and wrote to young Prince Charles: *'We know not but this may be the last time we may speak to you or the world publicly; we are sensible into what hands we are fallen…These men which have forced laws which they were bound to observe, will find their triumphs full of troubles.'*

The Thirty Years' War in Europe had now ended and the Queen began seeking help to save the King's life, (rather than his throne), but by the 24th November Charles was tired of fruitless negotiations with his enemies and sent them his final answer – he would never consent to the destruction of the Church of England and Book of Common Prayer. The missive was concluded with the text from *Mark*, Chapter 8: verse 36:-

"What is a man profited, if he shall gain the whole World and lose his own Soul?"

OPEN ANTAGONISM

Ireton was pleased – the King's final refusal removed the last obstacle for his attack on sovereignty. Whether Ireton was Cromwell's counsellor, mouthpiece, colleague or ally, is unclear, but they certainly held the same opinions and were already agreed that, because *'that Man of Blood'* had encouraged the second civil war, *'he must die.'*

Events then moved quickly: Ireton had already drawn up an army *Remonstrance*, setting out the reasons for bringing to justice a King who was a traitor to the *'people'*, ie. the army. The draft, (apparently approved on the 10th November), demanded *'That capitall and grand Author of our troubles, the person of the King by whose commissions, commands, or procurement, and in whose behalfe and for whose interest only (of will and power) all our warres and troubles have been (with all the miseries attending them), may be speedily brought to justice for the treason, blood and mischiefe he is therein guilty of.'*

In vain the Royalists remonstrated that it was *'Parliament which had taken the first steps towards civil war…first invited the Scots and that if Charles had rejected the proposals of Parliament to destroy the Church, Parliament had in turn, rejected his promise to modify the Establishment.'*

In their determination to secure supremacy over Crown, Church and Judiciary, the Council of Officers moved Charles to Hurst Castle (1st Dec.) *'without the knowledge or consent of Parliament.'* Fairfax staged a military coup the following day, drafting three thousand troops into the City to prevent anyone trying to bring back the King, but Colonel Thomas Pride *'purged'* opponents from the House of Commons and took over forty Presbyterian MPs prisoner, (apparently without orders from a furious Fairfax). Only a malleable Parliamentary 'rump' was left.

Fairfax was not a politician, but he voiced his disapproval of the parliamentary purge and arrest of the King, vowing to support Charles and Parliament as soon as they came to an agreement.

Cromwell and his army were parked outside Pontefract and it has been suggested that, like other times in his life, he was at the centre of events, but *'remained in the background until the stage was set'*. Judging that it was time to move, he left others to the prolonged seige and returned to London, where he was heard to say, *"I tell you, we will cut off his head with the crown on it."*

The Rump, (which now included many army officers and was responsible to the army instead of the nation), was instructed to find a way of trying the King. It needed to be something which looked legal and authoritive, because there was no provision in the Constitution for the Chief Executive of the Nation – a crowned and anointed monarch – to be tried in his own courts.

Charles was moved to Windsor, (23rd Dec.) where he was placed under double guard and Ireton and Cromwell issued a list of strict precautions in minutest detail. During that week, Cromwell also met with the Earl of Warwick, to discuss the possible danger from the new fleet which Prince Charles was preparing.

A *'Committee to consider how to proceed against the King and other capital offenders'* was formed and met on Christmas Day. Cromwell's proposal that the King's life could be spared if he accepted their conditions, was apparently passed, but six members still insisted on a trial and the results were put before the Commons, (probably on Boxing Day):-

"When it was first moved in the House of Commons to proceed capitally against the King, Cromwell stood up and told them, "Mr. Speaker, if any man whatsoever had carried on this design of deposing the King and disinheriting his posterity, or if any man had yet such a design, he should be the greatest traitor and rebel in the world. But since the Providence of God hath cast this upon us, I cannot but submit to Providence, though I am not yet provided to give you my advice."

It was responses such as this that divided people – they could not decide whether it was profound religious conviction, or profound dissimulation. Did he honestly believe he was guided by Divine Authority? Did he deceive himself, or was he deceiving others and using pretence as a means of avoiding responsibility? Even his supporters, who maintained that he *'was out of the ordinary'*, were troubled by this complex and elusive facet in his character. His letters would *'often suggest, rather than state his thoughts, which were wrapped in the mysteries of religious phraseology'* and left correspondents trying to read between the lines. Abbott considers that Cromwell's rise to prominence owed more to a combination of his military genius, political expertise and the ability to seize and make the most of opportunities as they occurred, maintaining that if anything had gone wrong, he could hardly have been convicted on semi-mystical pronouncements.

Whatever the truth, it served him well.

Cromwell was now moderating his behaviour – his *'rude, injudicious'* speeches were abandoned and he *'clothed his utterances in circumspection,'* adopting an almost ostentatious humility and meek *'submission to the will of God.'*

Suspicions that he was intent on seizing power for himself were growing.

ANNO DOMINI 1649.

On New Year's Day the Rump passed an ordinance to convene a new High Court of Justice – in effect a court-martial. The indictment agreed was that *'…it is Treason in the King of England for the time being to levy War against the Parliament and Kingdom of England.'*

Although there were only eleven Lords still in Parliament, two members in particular objected – the Earl of Manchester, who asserted that *"declaring the King a traitor was against every fundamental principle of law"* and the Earl of Northumberland, who agreed, saying:-

"Not one in twenty of the people in England are yet satisfied whether the king did levy war against the Houses first, or the Houses first against him; and, besides, if the King did levy war first, we have no law extant that can be produced to make it treason in him to do; and, for us, my Lords, to declare treason by an Ordinance when the matter of fact is not yet proved, nor any law to bring to judge it by, seems very unreasonable."

Bravely, the few Lords *'cast it out'* and then adjourned for a week to make it more difficult for the hot-heads to drive it forwards; but the Rump was not deterred. It suppressed the Lords, refused Henrietta Maria permission to visit her husband, made itself the supreme authority in the State, introduced a republic, (a 'Commonwealth of England'), and passed the *'Act of the Commons of England assembled in Parliament for the erecting of a High Court of Justice, for trying Charles Stuart, King of England.'*

The three Kingdoms were fast gaining an insight into what life would be like without a sovereign and the checks and balances of an Upper House. There was widespread censure and attendance in the Upper House shrank to an average of four. Mr. Prynne was investigated by the Rump, which demanded to know if he was responsible for a pamphlet referring to *'their lawful king'*, but he, (who had lost his ears under Charles), replied that he would answer only to a *'lawful authority.'*

TRIAL OF THE KING.

From the beginning, most of England's senior judiciary, (including the Solicitor General, the Chief Justice Oliver St. John, Widdrington and Sir Henry Vane), disassociated themselves from the proceedings and denounced it a *'judicial farce'*. William Steele of Gray's Inn, (the Attorney-General of the Commonwealth), had been selected to prosecute, but developed a convenient illness[46]; no Peers would lend their support and General Fairfax and most Army Commanders immediately absented themselves.

Only fifty-three commissioners, (or jurymen), turned up for their first planning meeting (8th) and the *'Mercurious Pragmaticus'* reported that Cromwell and Ireton made *'...his Excellency, [Fairfax]...a mere stalking horse for their designs and in effect but Deputy-General, upon courtesie, to carry on their present proceedings'*.

The rebels were making it up as they went along – with several senior judges having refused to serve, John Bradshaw, (who eventually presided), was probably the best they could come up with. He had recently been appointed serjeant-at-law and was a committed republican. The trial was to be conducted *'according to instructions to be given them by the 'Court'* and the commissioners

---

[46] Steele was involved in the prosecution of leading Royalist supporters a month later.

were to be judges, jury and prosecutors combined. Proclamations invited witnesses to give evidence against the King.

Abbott noted that the High Court of Justice, the remnant of the House and the Army Council had a *'closely allied membership'* and that thirty-one of the officers were commissioners. Therefore, as a member of the Army Council, a rump of a Commons and now the new High Court of Justice, Cromwell was a soldier, legislator and judge; very definitely at the centre of events and particularly active in the erection of the High Court of Justice, its organization and the conduct of the trial. (There are no surviving minutes of the Army Council's meetings between the 13th January and 22nd February. Either they did not keep records, or they were destroyed).

Fairfax was ordered to supply sufficient guards for the trial – Westminster Hall was swarming with soldiers as 230 men were ordered to prevent a public tumult and guard against the rescue, or escape of Charles. *'Neither Cromwell nor Fairfax went about without a guard of at least 300 horse'* and troops were stationed at strategic points in London and Westminster. The vaults under the Painted Chamber were investigated and secured – proceedings would be illegal and they were not going to risk another Gunpowder Plot.

It was generally felt that the verdict would be a foregone conclusion, so there were many attempts to prevent the trial and save the King's life. One petition presented to Fairfax – against the exclusion and imprisonment of the majority of the Commons, the seizure of the King and the proceedings of the army – included the signatures of forty-seven London Presbyterian Ministers. Ireton, particularly, was conscious that a large majority was just waiting for an opportunity to restore at least some of the old order. Rebel leaders were kept busy suppressing the rising opposition.

At his own request, Dr. Juxton was authorized *'to continue with the King in private, under the same restraint as the King is.'*

Charles was arrested and taken under heavy guard to Westminster by boat. As he disembarked, Cromwell turned *'as white as the wall'* and reportedly said to colleagues, "*My masters, he is come, he is come…let us resolve here what answer we shall give the King when he comes before us, for the first question he will ask us will be by what authority and commission do we try him?*" None answered, but presently Marten said, "*In the name of the Commons and Parliament assembled and all the good people of England.*"

Despite elaborate preparations, on the opening day of the trial, (20th Jan.), a 'safe' majority and 'weighty' judges were lacking. When the roll was called, Clarendon reported that Lady Fairfax answered on her husband's behalf, saying, ' *"He has more wit than to be here", [which] put the court into some disorder.'*

When Charles was led into Westminster Hall, (which was decked out with captured Royal Standards), it was to be tried *'as a traitor before a court which carried no authority [and he] cut an impressively regal figure'*. Despite being offered no legal assistance for defence, he conducted himself ably, questioned the legality of the court, refused to recognise it and laughed at the charge against him, i.e. that it was *'…out of a wicked design to erect and uphold in himself an unlimited and tyrannical power, to rule according to his will, and to overthrow the rights and liberties of the people,'* that he had *'traitorously and maliciously levied war against the present Parliament, and the people therein represented…[and had] renewed or caused to be renewed the war in 1648',* all of which, the charge concluded, *'have been, and are carried on for the advancement and upholding of a personal interest of will, power, and pretended prerogative to himself and his family, against the public interest, common right, liberty, justice and peace of the people of this nation.'*

Bradshaw, (who had taken the precaution of lining his beaver with steel and wearing armour under his robe), demanded that the King answer *'in the behalf of the Commons assembled in Parliament and the good people of England.'*

A masked woman, (again thought to be Lady Fairfax), immediately shouted out, *"It's a lie, not half, nor a quarter of the people in England! Oliver Cromwell is a rogue and a traitor."*

The guards were ordered to fire into the gallery, but they disobeyed and Lady Fairfax was persuaded to leave the Court. She had, however, put the majority's thoughts into words.

Reputed to be *'short tempered and long winded'*, Bradshaw then made the mistake of referring to Charles as an *elected* King and Charles, a King by inheritance, ran rings round him, reminding the court of the hereditary principle – he was a King not by election, for *"England was never an elective Kingdom: it was a hereditary Kingdom for near this thousand years."*

Bradshaw was cornered and he adjourned the court as Charles' military escort was encouraged to shout, *"Justice, Justice"* and the crowd contradicted, *"God save the King."*

On the second day, (22nd), Charles again maintained the upper hand; he questioned the court's legality, refused to co-operate and argued about *"the duty I owe to God in the preservation of true liberty of my people"*. *"How [he asked], can any free-born subject of England call life, or anything he possesseth his own, if power without right daily make new, and abrogate the old fundamental laws of the land?"* The proceedings against him, he continued, were warranted neither by the law of God nor of the land; the people <u>could</u> delegate such power to Parliament, but, he said, *"You have never asked the question of the tenth man in this Kingdom"*. He also questioned where the House of Commons acquired its authority, if not from the majority of the people, or how, without the King or Lords, could they pretend to make laws or erect a court? *"I speak"*, he continued, *"Not for my own right alone…but also for the true liberty of all my subjects, which consists not in the power of government, but in living under such laws, such a government, as may give themselves the best assurance of their lives, and property of their goods."*

Bradshaw ordered the King to be removed from the court.

Protests and appeals from Presbyterian clergy, Dutch ambassadors and Scots, (who had ignored Cromwell's request for their support[47]), continued. Even the Republicans thought the planned execution abhorrent.

On the third day, when Charles again claimed that he stood for the liberties of the people, Bradshaw instructed the clerk to record the King's guilt *'by default'*, adjourned the court and the King was hustled out. The 3rd, 4th and 5th days continued in the privacy of the Painted Chamber, but there were fears that Fairfax might use the army to effect a rescue, so Cromwell put a guard on him. Many witnesses were produced to give evidence that the King had levied war against his people and, with only forty-six commissioners present, they resolved that *'this court will proceed to sentence of condemnation against Charles Stuart, King of England…for tyrant, traitor and murtherer…for being a public enemy to the Commonwealth of England…that this vote shall extend to death'.* The vote, however, must have been considered unsatisfactory, because it was passed off as a *preliminary* opinion and renewed efforts were made to increase support. A further sixteen were persuaded to put in an appearance and after an amendment to omit the words *'high treason'*, the vote to execute the King *'by the severing of his head from his body'*, was carried.

On Saturday the 27th, Charles was again taken into court, amidst shouts of *"Justice and Execution"*, to listen to a tirade from Bradshaw about the court's *'past forebearance'* and be reminded

---

[47] Lt.-Gen. Drummond to Bishop Gilbert Burnett. Cromwell met members of the Scotch General Assembly in Oct. 1648, when he *'discoursed with them with a fair flourish of words and sometimes tears, saying that he "was for monarchical government and that in the person of this king and his posterity."* The moderator, Blair, subsequently remarked, *"If you knew him as well as I do, you would not believe one word he says. He is an egregious dissembler & a great liar. Away with him, he is a greeting [weeping] devil".*

that he had been called upon to answer *'in the name of the people of England.'*

Again there was an interruption from the gallery, as a masked lady shouted, *"Not half of the people, Oliver Cromwell is a traitor!"* When order was restored, Charles repeated his previous requests – that he be heard by the Lords and Commons, adding that he had taken his course on behalf of the people's liberties and not for his own advantage.

One of the commissioners, (Downes), stood up and said, *"I am not satisfied to give my consent to this sentence, but have reasons to offer you against it, and desire the Court may adjourn to hear me"*. He secured his adjournment, but was *'hissed down by a furious Cromwell,'* who claimed that they were dealing with *'the hardest-hearted man that lives upon the earth [and] it was not fit that the Court should be hindered from their duty by one peevish man…'* He then *'desired the Court, without any more ado would go and do their duty'*. They re-convened, refused the King's request and forbade him further speech. Following a further tirade from Bradshaw, the formal *Sentence of Death* was read. Charles tried to protest, but he was dragged out of Westminster Hall by guards who were again encouraged to shout, *"Justice, justice."*

Evidence suggests that the death-warrant was also rigged – that there was much coercion, (both in the Commons and in the Painted Chamber), and that the final vote was sharply divided. Certainly the date and three of the fifty-nine names on the document have been altered. The list includes nearly all of Cromwell's parliamentary relatives and there were reports that some, (including Cromwell and Marten), inked one another's faces like boisterous schoolchildren.

But they had trouble finding someone to execute the King. London continued on tenterhooks as people questioned the court's legality and what might be done to stop Cromwell and his associates. There were countless private objections as well as official protests from the Assembly of Divines, the States General, Louis XIV of France, Prince Charles and the Scots. (The rebels were so set on regicide that they had avoided debates with either Scots or Irish – Charles was their King also and their anger was understandable).

Everybody looked to Fairfax. There was a force of 20,000 ready to help him rescue the King, but it would appear that he was afraid of causing another very prompt, very bloody civil war. Instead he tried diplomatic means, *'using all in his power and interest to have the execution deferred.'*

THE EXECUTION

After sending tender messages to his wife, explaining to his children what would happen and, telling them to forgive his judges and executioner, the King prepared himself for the unknown as best he could, relying heavily on the doctrines of the Church of England.

On the morning of the execution, Fairfax and others were still endeavouring to get the decision overturned and, as opposition mounted, Cromwell said they should seek God's will in the matter. He then involved them all in long-winded prayer.

It was a bitter day, but Charles went to his death *'like a King,'* stating that his submission to the verdict did not signify guilt and that he died *"a Christian according to the Profession of the Church of England. I have a good cause,"* he said, *"and a gracious God."*

Bishop Juxon offered words of support and assurance:-

"There is but one stage more. This stage is turbulent and troublesome. It is a short one. But you may consider it, it will soon carry you a very great way. It will carry you from earth to heaven, and there you shall find your great joy, the prize. You haste to a crown of glory."

The King responded,

"I go from a corruptible to an incorruptible crown, where no disturbance can be."

Dr. Juxton replied, *"You are exchanged from a temporal to an eternal crown, a good exchange."*

As the axe struck home on 30th January, *'a deep groan rose from the crowd, a terrible sound'* which one shocked witness said he had never heard before and hoped never to hear again.

Cromwell's prayer was still on-going, when a messenger arrived to say that the deed was done and Fairfax realised that he had been *'overwitted'* by Cromwell.

The Church of England remembers *'Charles, King and Martyr'* on the anniversary of his execution.

THE COMMONWEALTH of ENGLAND

With the backing of the army, Cromwell and his small, unrepresentative group wasted no time. Two days later, with the country weary of war and the Royalists bewildered, frightened and appalled, the republic swung into action. Out went *'the office of King'*, the *'useless and dangerous'* House of Lords, the various Councils, the King's statue, all Royal arms and badges – in came a Council of State, (an executive body for the rump), a new Great Seal, lesser seals of office and coinage. The King's name was also removed from oath-taking and courts, whilst warships were re-named. All officials and armed forces throughout the British Isles were now under republican control.

Pulpits were frequently used to influence political beliefs and, as *'primus inter pares*[48]*',* of the Puritan rebellion, Cromwell engineered *'a network of [Independent] congregations throughout England which could be relied on to support them and keep them advised of their opponents' activities'.* But suspicions were again being voiced – was Cromwell now *'aspiring...towards a new regality?'*

A week after the King's execution, Edinburgh heard the news and proclaimed his eldest son King – Charles II of Great Britain, France and Ireland – his *father having been done to death by the traitorous parliament and army (all honest men being formerly removed').* They then put the country *'in a posture of defence'* and waited for the repercussions. (Jersey and Ireland also declared for the young King).

The European Monarchies were horrified by events in England, but they had been exhausted after the 'Thirty Years' War' and

---

[48] First amongst equals.

no practical help had been forthcoming for Henrietta Maria. She was particularly disappointed with the French monarchy.

RELIGIOUS RE-ORGANIZATION

Lancashire was one of the first counties to exchange Episcopacy for Presbyterianism, with its committees, (or Classis), comprising both lay persons and ordained. Here also, ministers were to be supported by the sequestration funds and in December 1649, Richard Smethurst was ordained as minister for Samlesbury @ £40 p.a., (plus arrears, because he had already served 20 weeks).

During August, Dr. Smith, (the absentee Vicar-Apostolic of the English Mission), introduced a ten-point code of conduct for *'the common good'* – to which John Southworth and thirteen others are known to have subscribed. He also appointed Rev. George Gage to be Vicar-General and Archdeacon for John's area. At that time John was based at the home of the Spanish ambassador, Alonso de Cardenas, and it would appear that he sometimes *'crossed swords'* with Gage, but Purdie could not discover why.

In 1650, the law enforcing attendance at the parish churches was repealed. It took pressure off Roman Catholics, but was actually an attack on the Established Church, (Reynolds).

State Puritanism was gradually taking over.

A THIRD CIVIL WAR

Young Charles Stuart, (1630-1685) had hoped for support from Ireland, but because Cromwell had ruthlessly crushed the Royalists there[49], he finally accepted an invitation to Scotland. With great reluctance, he signed the Covenant and arrived in

---

[49] In the Autumn of 1649 Cromwell had avenged the insurrection of 1641. He invaded Ireland and slaughtered the Royalist garrisons of Drogheda & Wexford. Then, disdaining the Irish and being contemptuous of Roman Catholicism, he exercised his authority as Lord Lieutenant of Ireland and *'replanted…with many noble families of this nation, and of the Protestant religion.'*

June 1650, to face indoctrination. Scots diarist Alexander Jaffray noted, *'We did both sinfully entangle and engage the nation, ourselves and that poor, young prince to whom we were sent, making him sign and swear a Covenant which we knew from clear and demonstrable reasons, that he hated in his heart.'*

Cromwell's spies heard that an insurrection to overthrow the Commonwealth was imminent and that Fairfax would aid the new King. It sounded ominous. Cromwell tried unsuccessfully to persuade Fairfax to lead a force to subdue the Scots – but the King's execution had disgusted Fairfax – he refused, resigned his commission and retired to his Yorkshire estates.

The Council of State commissioned Cromwell in his place and the repercussions began. Taking 16,000 men with him, Cromwell invaded Scotland in July 1650, defeated them at Dunbar on 3rd September and entered Edinburgh. Despite Cromwell being keen to win over the Scots by *'fair means, rather than punish them'*, the city's churches, school and college were still *'wasted'* and pulpits, desks, lofts, windows, doors, etc., knocked down by the New Model Army and *'burned to ashes'*. By the time the Castle surrendered on Christmas Eve, the New Model Army controlled both the Lowlands and the routes into England.

The Scots crowned Charles at Scone on New Year's Day 1651 – but did not anoint him – that would have been *'superstitious'* and *'popish'*. The news travelled and by May, Barbados, Bermuda, Antigua and Virginia had all declared for Charles II.

Cromwell suffered a long-term intermittent fever/ague during the winter and early summer, but in July 1651, he moved north, crossed the Forth and soundly beat the Scots at Inverkeithing. The survivors had one option left – whilst Cromwell was 'mopping up', they skirted round him and hurried south, planning to rally Royalist support and engage with the Parliamentary troops left in England. Charles was declared

King near Carlisle, (6th Aug), Penrith, (7th) and Lancaster (11th), but there was little support – many Royalists had been eliminated and there was antipathy towards Scots invaders. In addition, the Scots' *Solemn League and Covenant* was being imposed on all Royalists and it was a big obstacle south of the Border. Potential supporters, including most of the gentry, were unwilling to sign.

With his usual efficiency, Cromwell left General Monck to complete the subjugation of Scotland, followed the Royalists south and, exactly a year after Dunbar, defeated them at Worcester – the last major battle of the civil wars. About 3,000 Royalists were killed and 10,000 Scots were sold into slavery in New England, Bermuda and the Caribbean.

As Charles made his dispirited way back to France, he was recognized many times; but despite the offer of a reward, he was never betrayed and his narrow escapes, (including hiding in an oak tree at Boscobel), passed into folk lore.

'HIS HIGHNESS OLIVER CROMWELL, the LORD PROTECTOR'

Cromwell dissolved the rump Parliament in April 1653, whilst the Council of Officers adopted an *'Instrument of Government'* and appointed their *'nominated'*, or *'Barebones'* Parliament.

The Independents were in the ascendant and many of their supporters were nominated to serve; their churches/sects were re-organized and they then *'largely enjoyed the [Anglican] emoluments.'* In December Cromwell was invested with the title, *'His Highness Oliver Cromwell, Lord Protector of the Commonwealth of England, Scotland and Ireland and the dominions and territories thereunto belonging';* Royal properties were refurbished, (and in some cases, repurchased), for the use of the Cromwells and visiting dignitaries; gardens were re-designed and pieces of the royal collection were brought out of storage for display.

Cromwell's authority seemed secure – he had leadership qualities, worked hard and was well acquainted with the British Isles, but many resented the way he had used them as he progressed to the top; the press was firmly censored, the amy's protection was imperative and the execution of the King had not led to peace or changed anything for the better.

CHAPTER III

REV. JOHN SOUTHWORTH: JULY 1653 ONWARDS

MISSIONARY DEVELOPMENT OF THE SECULARS

Although Cromwell conducted his foreign policy with considerable aggression, the first few months of the Protectorate were surprisingly successful, and it was whilst he and his Party were busy consolidating their position, that the Seculars convened in London on 11th July. There was to be an eight-day General Assembly and delegates travelled in from many parts of England and Wales.

The Vicar-Apostolick had now been absent about twenty-four years and the Dean and Chapter were still keeping everyone going as best they could. There had been no official recognition from Rome[50] and improvements were desperately needed. Discussions, therefore, included the possible establishment of permanent self-supporting missions and ways of increasing efficiency. Officers needed to be appointed and maintenance found for them, (for which John Southworth and a colleague were detailed to collect £25 in London, Westminster and Middlesex[51]).

They also debated Dr. Smith's ten-point code of conduct, which included obedience to the Pope, dealing with difficult situations and their own conduct towards each other. Better provision was essential for both those in prison and for those arriving in England without *'competent friends or Patrimony'*. There was also the question of financial obligations to the *'Body of the Secular clergy'*, when they themselves died and it was agreed that, should the common purse fail, collections would have to be taken.

---

[50] Archer.
[51] Westminster Archives: XXX, 559 quoted by Purdie.

THE QUESTIONABLE 'GERARD-VOWELL CONSPIRACY'

When Thurloe[52] and his intelligencers reported yet another plot to assassinate Cromwell in May 1654, they believed it emanated from the exiled followers of Henrietta Maria. (Certainly the alleged ringleader, John Gerard[53], had met Charles II on the continent). Cromwell, however, had always considered the Papacy and the Jesuits to be the chief threats to European peace and this, he felt, was being directed by Cardinal Mazarin, who had studied at the Jesuit College in Rome and was now the Chief Minister of the French Court. Accordingly, letters between England and the continent were intercepted and the following six weeks were devoted to investigations, detentions, arrests and searches for arms and ammunition.

Lorenzo Paulucci, (who was also becoming hostile to the Protector), reported that many in London hoped for his overthrow and it was rumoured that the Cardinal was offering 200,000 livres reward to the successful assassin – two priests and Prince Rupert's surgeon were believed to have been lined up for the job.

By the 1st June, sufficient evidence had been gathered and enough plotters were under arrest to go for trial. Having successfully usurped the King, Cromwell would then be defending his position tooth and nail – on the 6th he ordered the arrest of two further suspects, followed by an ordinance for the apprehension of priests and Jesuits on the 7th:-

---

[52] Thurloe ran an extraordinarily successful intelligence service. He was paid £800 in May and £600 eight months later. (In the course of his work, they also infiltrated the court of Chas.II).
[53] Gerard was a young Lancastrian who had been an ensign in the King's army & Peter Vowell, (see next page), kept a boys' school in Islington.

'To [Major] John White

Whereas We are informed that several priests and Jesuits are now resident in this Commonwealth, contrary to the laws in that case provided: These are to require and authorize you to apprehend all such persons whom you know to be priests, or Jesuits, and them forthwith to bring before Our Council at Whitehall. And for the better performing of the premisses all constables, and other officers are hereby required to be aiding, and assisting you.'

In preparation for the prosecution of the Gerard-Vowell plotters, an ordinance was issued for a *High Court of Justice* on the 13th June, and this was followed on the 16th by an order for the seizure of Jesuits and nuns. It would be the two orders regarding priests, Jesuits and nuns which caused one witness to comment,

"Priests fly hence apace, as presaging a greater storm. There are others in hold, and search made after more. All are in fears and suspense, not knowing where to dispose themselves, the times are so hard..." (Challoner).

Knaresborough reported a brief encounter between John Southworth and Dr. Leyburne, which may also have been connected to this London exodus. It was shortly before John's final arrest and the president was on his way back to Douay: John *'desired with great earnestness to accompany him into Flanders and spend the remainder of his life in retirement, being then very old,'* but the President refused his request, saying that he *"would not deprive the nation of so zealous a missioner."*

"Well Sir," John replied, *"If you will not let me go with you, at least I'll follow you.*[54]*"*

---

[54] G. Anstruther: *The Seminary Priests:* Knaresborough took this from Mr. Augustine Smithson, (Aug. 1706), who had it from Dr. Leyburne himself. (Perhaps John had already made provisional arrangements with the Howards, for the disposal of his earthly remains). Anstruther also notes that the Venetian Ambassador in London said John was 70 years old when he was executed.

John would certainly be feeling old, having spent much of his working life on an emotional roller-coaster. He had had a death sentence hanging over him for twenty-seven years, experienced stressful work amongst the poor and plague-stricken, and lost a number of colleagues to the gibbet. John would have benefitted from some rest and compassion.

THE FINAL ARREST OF JOHN SOUTHWORTH

Instead, Lieutenant-Colonel Charles Worsley JP[55], (who had already seized several of the Gerard-Vowell conspirators), questioned a pursuivant named Jefferies[56], learned of John's whereabouts and then searched his lodgings. They found *'in his chamber all the requisites for the celebration of the Mass, to which he intrepidly owned, [and] compelled him to get up [out of bed] and carried him off prisoner.*[57]*'*

The Gaol Delivery Rolls record that John was arrested on Monday 19th June 1654, (2nd of the Protectorate) and charged with being a seminary priest:-

S' JOHN SOUTHWORTH

pro. *Seminar. Sacerdot.*

The indictment, (or Jurors' Oath), reads:-

The Jurors of the Lord Protector of the Commonwealth of England, Scotland, and Ireland etc., upon their oath doe present that John Southworth late of the parish of Giles-in-the-Fields in the county of

---

[55] The Lancastrian Puritan who was ordered by Cromwell to clear the MPs from the Commons and remove the *'bauble'*; (the Mace). So he took it home. Worsley became Cromwell's second-in-command in 1655 and Major-General for the Lancs., Ches. and Staffs., region, until his death 'from overwork', in 1656. Ironically, Worsley, (1612-1656), is buried in Westminster Abbey, whilst his prey lies in Westminster Cathedral.

[56] John would be paying Jefferies to leave him alone, because Jefferies had John *'in fee'*. (Challoner quoting a St. Omer's MS.).

[57] Venetian State Papers, No. 287: Purdie quoting a letter from Paulucci to the Venetian Ambassador in Paris in 1654.

Middlesex clerke was borne within England.....And before the nineteenth day of June in the yeare of Oure Lord one thousand six hundred fifty fower in the parts beyond the seas was made and ordayned a Preist [sic] by authority derived and pretended from the Sea of Rome And that the aforesayd John Southworth the lawes and statutes of England little weighinge, nor the paine in them conteyned anie waies fearing the aforesaid nineteenth day of June in the said yeare of our Lord one thousand six hundred fifty fower from the parts beyond the seas aforesaid unto the Common Wealth of England to witt att the said parish of Giles-in-the-fields in the county aforesayd on the said nineteenth day of June in the year aforesaid traiterously and as a false traitor to this Commonwealth of England did stay was and did remayne Against the forme of the statute in such case made and provided and against the publique peace.'

On the reverse are four names – Stephen Shalcross, Robert Brooks, John Woodworth and Jeoffrey Ellison – presumably members of the Grand Jury, who had considered the indictment and decided that there was sufficient evidence to go for trial. (As John had already admitted priesthood, the evidence was established), and the *Entries of Session* record that on Wednesday 21st June, he was committed to Newgate Gaol, (which was next door to the Sessions House), for trial on Saturday 24th:-

JOHN SOUTHWORTH

for a Secular popish priest

(before Justice Worsley).

JOHN'S TRIAL

John's final trial was at London's senior court, the Sessions House in the Old Bailey. It was not a new case – it was the re-visiting and re-sentencing of the 1627 conviction and the 1630 perpetual banishment order.

John pleaded *not guilty* to treason, but acknowledged that he was *"a priest of the Roman church"* and had been a condemned man for many years[58].

The penal laws, which had been needed to maintain national security since Tudor times, were still in place, but foreign threats were subsiding and the attitudes of many were changing. Following his admission, *'it clearly appeared that those who were his judges[59] did their utmost to preserve his life, and to prevent the execution against him of those laws upon which he stood indicted ; for they did for many hours suspend the recording of his confession, making it their endeavour to prevail with him to plead "not guilty" to the indictment. They pressed him to this in the public court, assuring him that if he would so plead his life should be safe, and that they had no evidence which could prove him to be a priest'.* However, it could not be – even though nobody had given evidence against him, he had admitted priesthood and John, like the King, would not renege on his deeply held beliefs.

Sergeant William Steele[60] was now the senior permanent judge of the Central Criminal Court, (1649-1655) and on Monday the 26th June, John *'was agayne called to the bar and had the sentence of death pronounced against him[61]...'* For some time Steele *'was so drowned in tears…that it was long before he could pronounce the sentence which the law compelled [him] as he professed, to give:-'*

---

[58] *A Letter from a gentleman in the city to a gentleman in the country, about the odiousness of persecution*: Westminster Archives Vol. XXX, p.635, quoted by Purdie: Writing a letter to a 'friend' was one of Cromwell's ways of influencing the public though the pamphleteers. It may have been written by John Hall, who was on Cromwell's pay roll, because a pamphlet known to have been written by him, entitled, *'A Letter written to a Gentleman in the Country, in defence of the dissolution of the late Parliament',* was likewise signed *'N. LL'* - the last letters of each of his names.

[59] Others were entitled to sit with the Recorder, so magistrates may also have been present.

[60] Abbott: As Recorder for the City of London, Wm. Steele MP. JP., was chosen to welcome the new Lord Protector to the City with a laudatory speech, but he spoke for much of the time about the origin of government and the duties of rulers. Cromwell conferred the honour of Sergeant-at-Law on him in 1653/4 & he went on to become Baron of the Exchequer (1655), Lord Chancellor of Ireland (1656) and was one of 5 Commissioners appointed to govern Ireland in 1659, where *'he conducted himself with great prudence and uncorrupted integrity.'*

[61] Purdie, quoting Westminster Archives, Volume XXX, p.635.

"You shall be taken back to the prison from whence you were brought, thence you shall be drawne to the place of execution and there hanged by the neck until thou art half-dead: your head shall then be cut off and the rest of your members divided into four parts shall be fixed up at the four usual points of the city[62], and may God have mercy upon you!"

John then asked for a few words with the Court, said a brief prayer and thanked them for their civilities, praying that both they and the nation would become converts to Roman Catholicism *"and remaine in Heaven for ever with Jesus Christ in glory;"* to which the Recorder replied, *"Sir, wee thanke you, and will joyne with you in the latter part."*

After the sentence of death was passed, a prison clerk, (this is different handwriting), has set the *'sinister 'S'* (**S'**) beside John's name in the gaol register[63] and below his name at the top of the indictment has added, *po/ se/ cul/ ca/ null/ S'*, ie:-

ponit se = He puts himself on a jury;   *culpabilis* = found guilty; *catella nulla* = no property;   S' = suspendatur = let him be hanged.

At the bottom is appended:- *'the said John Southworth adjudged to be drawne, hanged and quartered, to witt etc.'* G.D.R. [Gaol Delivery Rolls], 1654.

---

[62] Purdie, as above. (Remains were sometimes thrown into a huge pit beside the gallows: *Guide to the Crypt of Martyrs:* Tyburn Convent).
[63] Purdie, quoting Middlesex County Records, Vol. III, p. 225. Cfr. Westminster Guildhall, Session Rolls, No. 1125/9. (See Royal Warrant extract, p.23)

✝ The next day, (27ᵗʰ), whilst William Steele was involved in organizing the new High Court of Justice, for the trial of the alleged Gerard-Vowell ringleaders⁶⁴, vigorous efforts were being made by the foreign ambassadors⁶⁵ to gain John a reprieve.

Diarist and antiquarian Richard Symonds, recorded that Cromwell, who had *'disavowed responsibility for the execution of King Charles',* had also appeared averse to John's barbaric death sentence and told the Portuguese Ambassador⁶⁶, *"God forbid [my] hand should be consenting to the death of any for religion"* and promised a reprieve.

But Cromwell's assurance accorded neither with his own ordinances for the arrest of priests, nuns and Jesuits, nor with the *'Instrument of Government',* in which it was stated that the Protector's *'power of pardons [did not include] cases of murder, or treason...'* Cromwell knew that pardon was not his to give – he could not set the law aside. His promise was only a means of getting them out of his hair and the next morning a messenger reneged on it⁶⁷.

---

⁶⁴ *State Trials, 6 Charles II.* A High court, (which infringed ancient law), had been erected because juries were becoming unmanageable. Gerard and Vowell were remanded until the 4ᵗʰ July and executed on 10ᵗʰ. Somerset Fox, the third alleged leader, was sentenced to transportation. Steele also tried the Portuguese Ambassador's brother. It was a complicated case – he had committed murder and then tried to claim diplomatic immunity as a bar to trial by an English court. He too was executed on the 10ᵗʰ.
⁶⁵ Cardenas' communication to Cromwell: Thurloe ii 376, note.
⁶⁶ Whitworth: Schofield & Skinner: John's immediate superior appears to have lodged with the Portuguese Ambassador and sided against Spain on political issues.
⁶⁷ Although back in 1648, Cromwell had written that he *'desired from his heart',* overall toleration for *'godly people'* (Scots, English, Jews, Gentiles, Presbyterians, Independents and Anabaptists), Roman Catholics and Episcopalians did not rate a mention. Paulicci, however, reported in 1653 *'that Cromwell intended that for the future only murderers should suffer capital punishment.'*

EXECUTION

On Wednesday 28th, John Southworth, *'cloathed in a priest's gown and four-cornered cap,'* was fastened down on a hurdle between two coiners[68] and bumped along two miles of rough roads to Tyburn Fields, (a place of public executions for nearly 600 years). This journey along the 'execution route' could take anything up to three hours.

A severe thunderstorm soon had them covered in mud and the French Ambassador wrote that *'he was attended to the place of execution by two hundred coaches, and a great many people on horseback, who all admired his constancy'.* Hundreds of foot followers were also reported, as well as the many who watched from windows and rooftops.

A priest was usually the last to be executed, so John probably had to watch several others being put to death[69], before he himself *'mounted the fatal carte'* and, as Paulucci says, was proclaimed *'a papist, a seducer of the people and a disturber of the peace before an immense multitude of spectators...'*

---

[68] By clipping bits of gold off legal coins and melting them down, an opportunist could counterfeit others e.g. French, Spanish & Portuguese money was all legal tender in England.
[69] Purdie: *The Perfect Diurnal,* (Parliament's record of proceedings), for 28th June 1654, (No. 238, p.3647, British Museum): says, *'This day was executed at Tyburn nine men and one Woman',...* Challoner quotes 5 coiners and Paulucci says he was executed with 12 other criminals. Purdie also states that John looked 10 years older than he actually was. Reynolds notes another lull in executions between 1654 & 1678.

Like the King, John met his end with dignity and calm. In his long, last speech[70] he recounted that it was the third time he had been apprehended, [indicted and arraigned]. Three times he refers to Cromwell, denying that he had ever acted against the secular government, or meddled in temporal affairs. Although non-political, John took the opportunity to remind the Protector that justice should be administered impartially and equally and pointed out that he was not pleading for himself, but for the *'poor[71], persecuted Catholics'* he was leaving behind.

When he was told to hurry up, he asked the Roman Catholics in the crowd to pray for him, then passively waited to be hanged, drawn and quartered – the last Secular priest to be executed under the sentence of high treason at Tyburn and the only one during the rule of Cromwell.

It was also on that day that the Army Council ordered the City's garrison to be increased to an estimated total of 10,000 soldiers. It gave further protection to Cromwell, themselves and their own position.

RETURN to DOUAY

Cardenas bought John's quartered remains from the executioner for forty shillings, (£2.00) and a surgeon, Mr. James Clark, carefully stitched them back together and embalmed the whole, before, (according to Challoner), it was sent over to Douay *'...by one of the illustrious family of the Howards of Norfolk...'* In June 1655 Dr. Leyburn wrote to Pope Alexander VII to say that, *'quite recently two English Catholics of the highest Rank had sent the entire body of this grand martyr laid up in rich spices to the College.'* [72] Three

---
[70] This extract is from Westminster Archives XXX 635. Challoner's account, Westminster Archives XXX 636, is reproduced on p.105.
[71] John was using the word 'poor' as in pious & persecuted, rather than poverty-stricken.
[72] Purdie: Possibly the Dowager Countess of Arundel and her son Thos. Howard, the Earl. Their castle was ruined during the civil wars, so they were living in London. (Their Dukedom of Norfolk was restored in 1660 by Chas.II and in time two of the brothers inherited). John's body is not quite entire: the crown of the head would be removed during the embalming process and the ears and hands are also missing, probably having been

months later he was recording that the locals were '...*constantly, day by day, kneeling at the tomb, pouring out their prayers, and waxen images of different shapes are put up there by them in token of the different cures which the faithful people attribute to the intercession of the blessed martyr.*'

John had indeed followed the President to Douai.

His body remained in the chapel until the French Revolution, when British establishments were suppressed. Revolutionaries occupied the college in 1793, but staff and students managed to secrete silver plate, John's casket and other relics, before they could be plundered or destroyed. The buildings were soon used for other purposes and many records are thought to have been lost.

An attempt to recover the relics in 1863 yielded the silver plate, but no trace of the '*Venerable John Southworth.*' However, changes to part of the town's infrastructure in 1926 saw the college demolished, a road cut diagonally across the site and the adjacent land sold for development. John's lead casket, (about five feet eight inches long), was unearthed on 15th July 1927, at a site designated for a shop – the only building needing deep excavation for a cellar.

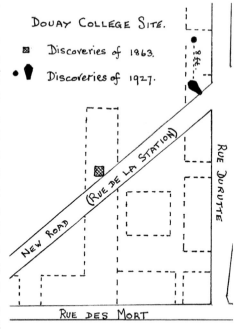

---

removed on his death & kept as relics. His right forearm and left clavicle were retained at Douai when he was returned to England.

CONFIRMATION of IDENTITY

An examination of the coffin's occupant proved that no expense had been spared with the embalming process and that Dr. Clark had used Philbert Guybert's preservation method of 1629. (Purdie).

John's face had taken on a coppery tint and his slight moustache and beard, (*'à la Richelieu'*), was chestnut, with no sign of grey. The teeth were also in good condition, but water seepage had caused deterioration to the chest and stomach. X-rays revealed that the body had been violently quartered and stitched back together.

In September, the Benedictines found a plan and other documents in their archives which referred to *'Mr. Southworth's body in the [old malt] kilnes exactly in the middle – six feet deep.'*

The plan also marks the position of other relics buried nearby, which were recovered the day after the casket, so it was proved beyond doubt that these were the remains of John Southworth. He was re-embalmed, brought back to England in December 1927 and entrusted to St. Edmund's College, Ware, where Father Purdie was headmaster.

In December 1929, John Southworth was one of a 136 who were beatified[73] by Pope Pius XI in St. Peter's Basilica, Rome. It was the first step towards canonization[74] and celebrations were also held in Westminster Cathedral and St. Edmund's College.

The following April, John's remains were moved to Westminster Cathedral, (travelling via Tyburn Convent, which is close to the execution site), and the following day a triduum[75] commenced with a solemn Mass. In 1954 his body was attired in contemporary red vestments, a four-cornered cap and shoes. A

---

[73] A formal declaration that the deceased displayed such an extent of holiness in their life, that they were worthy of public veneration.
[74] To declare & admit the deceased to the Canon of Saints.
[75] Three days of prayer & preparation for a Feast Day.

silver face mask and hands were added and he is now enclosed in a glass and bronze feretory[76].

CANONIZATION

On St. Peter's Day (25th Oct.) AD 1970, John Southworth was one of forty who were canonized by Pope Paul VI in St. Peter's Basilica, Rome. Pope Paul declared that they were *'worthy to stand alongside the greatest martyrs of the past...'* and for the first time, hymns from the Anglican tradition were used at a Papal Mass in Rome[77]. The Service was sung by Westminster Cathedral choir.

In November, local members of the Southworth family were present at a special Triduum of Thanksgiving in Westminster Cathedral and also at a crowded Service held in the great hall at Samlesbury Higher Hall.

John was adopted as co-patron of Samlesbury R.C. Chapel and in time the Roman Catholic Deanery of Blackburn and Ribble Valley, was also named after him.

Amongst 'The Forty' John is unique – he was the only one to admit priesthood and his are the only remains which have been preserved substantially intact from penal times until the 21st century.

Many have claimed healing through intercession to the Samlesbury saint, including the Honourable Francis Howard[78], (the second of the three brothers who were studying at Douay when John's body arrived). Francis became dangerously ill in 1656, *'...only not quite dead,'* and the College President, (remembering that *'it was this youth's brother sent us our Blessed Martyr's body'*), addressed prayers to him and Francis recovered, much to the amazement of the *'learnedest and greatest [medical] practitioners of the [Douai] University.'* Another instance

---

[76] A portable shrine.
[77] Schofield & Skinner.
[78] Purdie, from *Westminster Archives XXXI 335*. Account given by Rev. T. Progers, Prof. of Divinity 1655-1657.

occurred in the 1950s, when his relic at Samlesbury was applied to a lady's cancer-infected shoulder. When the medical board met to discuss the Relatio in May 1969, Mrs. Matthewman's cure was submitted in support of the Canonization of the 'Forty English and Welsh Martyrs.'

Evidence that the cure occurred in the context of invocation of the martyrs was subsequently accepted and on her death a few years later, the post-mortem revealed no trace whatsoever of fibro-sarcoma.

IN CONCLUSION

James Croston, the author of *'The History of the Ancient Hall of Samlesbury' (1871)*, commented, *'The liberty of conscience which Puritans had required for themselves, was not extended to others during the Commonwealth, the execution of Southworth furnishes a sad commentary on the state of religious freedom in England during the Usurpation…'*

Even Milton, (Cromwell's propagandist), when writing his *Second Defence of the English People,* urged his readers to disregard *'those who never fancy themselves free unless they deprive others of their freedom…'*

Surprisingly, John Southworth's final speech was published twenty-five years after his execution, when Titus Oates (1649-1705) fabricated a *'popish plot'* against the king. (Reynolds). Oates had an unsavoury past and the invented plot was supposedly aimed at assassinating Charles II, burning London, massacring the Anglicans and putting Charles' Roman Catholic brother, James, on the throne, supported by a Roman Catholic government. The 'plot' resulted in the deaths of 18 innocent people and his speech was published under the title, *'The Last Speech & Confession of Mr. John Southworth A popish priest at his execution at Tyburn June 28th, 1654.'*

It was printed for Henry Brome, agent for Roger L'Estrange, (an Anglican aristocratic English journalist), who, along with the king, was very sceptical of the plot's existence. Amidst all the frenzy he was afraid to voice his opinions, so published several tracts instead, hinting that there was more *'roguery than honesty in Oates and his gang'*. Oates turned on L'Estrange (1680) and he fled to Scotland, but the journalist was rewarded five years later with a knighthood, for helping to discredit the perpetrators. Perhaps by publicizing the speech of a Roman Catholic priest, who showed such firm support for the establishment, it was hoped to diffuse some of the hysteria which the supposed plot had aroused.

John knew he was breaking the law by remaining in England, in order to exercise the Roman Catholic ministry, but his point was that he was not a political activist, seeking to undermine the political system.

Purdie's opinion that Saint John Southworth *'appears to have been outside the intrigues that distracted many of his fellow missionaries'*, is hardly surprising – John would have experienced damaging religious schism at first hand, amongst his own relatives[79].

Memories were long and restoration of trust, slow, but Charles II's policy was to live and let live, as long as his authority was accepted. Both he and James II attempted to suspend the Penal Laws with Declarations of Indulgence in 1672 and 1687 respectively.

In 1689 the Act of Toleration was applied to Non-Conformists who rejected the teaching of transubstantiation and accepted the Oaths of Allegiance and Supremacy. The Moravian Church was recognised by Act of Parliament in 1749 and the Test & Corporation Acts were repealed for everyone except Roman Catholics in 1828. The final restrictions were lifted by the Catholic Emancipation Act of 1829.

---

[79] *The Famous Witches of Samlesbury:* G. Clayton.

Samlesbury's Saint John Southworth is still considered to be *'a model for every priest today'* and relics are kept in various places, including Samlesbury's R.C. Chapel, Tyburn Convent and Westminster Cathedral where, day by day, devotion to St. John Southworth continues.

The Saint John Southworth Caritas Funds, (a social action agency included in *Caritas Westminster*), is very much part of Westminster Cathedral life and continues the pastoral care for the marginalized which John practised in the 17th century.

His Feast Day is celebrated on 27th June.

Almost four hundred years have passed since John Southworth was executed and our Christian climate is now far removed from those bitter struggles of the 17th century.

Christians, however, still need to remember how costly our freedom of worship was to our forebears and how strenuously it was fought for, on all sides of the Anglican/Roman Catholic/Non-Conformist divide.

The ecumenical endeavours begun in the 20th century are now helping us to work together – we are on the same side and need the strength of Christian Unity to fight against the very evil forces working against Christianity in the world today.

> Our Christian Faith therefore, must be proclaimed boldly, because the way of **Christ** is the way of **Peace**.

APPENDIX

DOUAI, or Douay, (the English spelling of the name of the college), was in Flanders and was sponsored by the King of Spain, the Pope and Cardinal Allen. (Purdie).

A number of the Southworths trained at Douay; eg. Richard Southworth, (one of five brothers to study there), took charge of the original piece of tape from around St. John's coffin, became Prof. of Divinity and Vice-President, before he joined the English Mission in 1786 – and Thomas Southworth, (one of four brothers), who became President of Sedgeley Park from 1781-1816.

Where *'Henry de Southworth of Salmesbury Hall'* was trained and ordained is unknown, but he appears in the list of Vicars & Rectors of Blackburn, from 1501 to 1506.

The ALUMNUS OATH was as follows:-

'I, John Southworth, an Alumnus of the English College at Douay, considering the divine benefits which I have received, particularly that which has led me from my country now afflicted with heresy, and which has made me a member of His Catholic Church, desiring moreover to show myself not altogether unmindful of such great mercy of God, have resolved to offer myself to His divine service, so far as I am able for furthering the end of this College ; and I promise and swear before Almighty God that I am ready and will be ever ready, so far as His most holy grace shall help me, to receive Holy Orders in due time and to return to England in order to gain the souls of others as often and when it shall seem good to the Superior of this College so to command. In the meantime while I dwell here I promise to live peaceably and quietly, and manfully to obey the constitutions and rules of the College.' (Purdie).

The OATH of ALLEGIANCE was introduced after the Gunpowder Plot against King James I and Parliament. If the plot had been successful, it would have killed the king, most of the Anglican aristocracy and senior bishops of the Church of England. A Papal Bull was issued in 1606 enjoining English Catholics not to take this oath, or attend Anglican Services and Purdie says that the Archpriest, George Blackwell, subscribed to the Oath in 1608 and Rome deprived him of office.

Both James and his son, Charles I, considered the deposing power claimed by the pope to be a serious obstacle to loyalty. Consequently the Oath contained the sentence, '*...further, I do swear that I do from my heart abhor, detest & abjure as impious and heretical, this damnable doctrine and position, that princes excommunicated or deprived by the pope may be deposed or murdered by their subjects, or any whatsoever. And I do believe and in conscience am resolved, that neither the pope nor any person whatsoever, hath power to absolve me of this oath...*'

The OATH of ABJURATION[80]

'I do abjure and renounce the Pope's Supremacy and Authority over the Catholic Church in General, and over myself in Particular, And I do believe that there is not any Transubstantiation in the Sacrament of the Lords Supper, or in the Elements of Bread and Wine after Consecration thereof, by any Person whatsoever; And I do also believe that there is not any Purgatory, Or that the consecrated Host, Crucifixes, or Images, ought to be worshipped, or that any worship is due unto them; And I also believe that Salvation cannot be Merited by Works, and all Doctrines in affirmation of the said Points; I do abjure and renounce, without any Equivocation, Mental Reservation, or secret Evasion whatsoever, taking the words by me spoken, according to the common and usual meaning of them. So help me God.'

---

[80] Wikipedia/Abjuration

EXTRACT from the BASILIKON DORON,
by KING JAMES VI & I.

'Being born to be a king you are rather born to ONUS than HONOS: not excelling all your people so far in rank and honour, as in daily care and hazardous pains-taking for the dutiful administrations of that great office that God has laid upon your shoulders: laying a just symmetry and proportion between the height of your honourable place and the heavy weight of your great charge, and consequently in case of failure (which God forbid) of the sadness of your fall, according to the proportion of that height.'

THE BOOK OF COMMON PRAYER

The Book of Common Payer was the first official liturgy of the English Church and was intended for use throughout the country. Although it has been revised a number of times, it was originally drawn up in 1549 by Thomas Cranmer, a leader of the English Reformation. The book is a scheme of reading to aid understanding and study of the Bible and the two are inextricably linked.

THE PETITION[81] CIRCULATED by JOHN SOUTHWORTH and HENRY MORSE in 1636:-

TO THE CATHOLICKES OF ENGLAND
RIGHT HONOURABLE, RIGHT WORSHIPFULL, AND MUCH RESPECTED,

We underwritten being appointed to serve the infected Catholicks of the Citty and Suburbs of London, with our spiritual assistance, having seen with our eyes the extreme necessity which many of the poorer sort are fallen into, by reason of the present sickness, do thinke ourselves obliged

---
[81] (Westminster Archives XXVIII, 545)

even in conscience, to make the same knowne unto you, by a publicke letter, to the end that those, whom God hath ble'st with sufficient ability and meanes, taking so weighty a matter into their serious consideration, may, through the help of his holy grace, resolve with themselves forthwith, to do what in them lieth, and what in such an exigent Christian charity and duty bindeth everyone unto, for the necessary support and relief of so great a multitude.

  Wee do protest unto you seriously, even upon our soules and consciences, that the greatnesse of this calamitie exceedeth all belief, in so much as wee should never have imagined in the least part, of that which really is, had not our owne eyes, and daily experience attested the same unto us, and wee may truly averre, that this is so great a desolation amongst our poore brethren, joyned with the small meanes and power wee have, to relieve them, is a farre more grievous affliction unto us than all the labours and dangers, which wee undergoe daily for their spirituall ayde and comfort.

  There are some persons in the number of these afflicted, who, notwithstanding they were well borne, and bred, having beene constrained, through extremity of want, to sell, or pawne all they had, remaine shut up within the bare walls of a poore chamber, having not wherewithall to allay the rage of hunger, nor scarcely to cover nakednesse. There are others, who for the space of three dayes togeather have not gotten a morsell of bread to put into their mouths. Wee have just cause to fear, that some doe perish for want of food : others for want of tendance : others for want of ordinary helpes and remedies, with which they might easily escape death, and be cured. At this present there are above fifty severall families, which are visited and shut up : and truly such is the feeling, which many of these poore creatures have, of this their most wretched state, that finding themselves deprived of meanes whereby to live (all manner of work fayling them at this time), they are brought even to the brinke of despaire, wishing from their heart to be ceaz'd upon with the sicknesse (if God were so pleased) thereby to hasten death, and with it, the end of this their languishing paine, which to them is worse than death it selfe.

    The example of the Protestants, both in the Citty and the Countrey (which is well knowne to all) may bee no small inducement unto Catholicks to imitate their care, providence and bounty in this behalfe. We have heard of some particulars amongst them, which are very memorable. One noble man of theirs hath bestowed lately the summe of three hundred pounds, leaving it to the distribution of a Gentleman of good quality, who tooke the paines to visit the houses of the poore himselfe, and to divide it amongst them with his owne hands. An other party of account (Sonne to an Alderman of London) hath been seene to goe in person to seeke out the poore that wanted worke, being neighbours to such as were infected, and with his owne hands to bestow a large benevolence amongst them. And if those who acknowledge no merit in good workes, out of a generous minde, or naturall compassion are so ready to assist their distressed brethren so plentifully : it may seeme that no lesse, but rather much more should bee expected at the hands of Catholicks, who professing to believe the doctrine of merit[82], have thereby a farre higher motive than Protestants have to performe workes of Charity, and to open the bowells of mercy, especially in a time of so generall and pressing necessity, towards their poore and desolate brethren, who have no expectation of hope or relief from any, but from them alone.

---

[82] RC doctrine taught that salvation came by acquiring merit in the eyes of God, but Martin Luther's influence would still be very strong at that time. He had taught that mankind is saved by mercy alone, not by merit and it was this doctrine of *'justification by faith,'* to which John & Henry were referring when they wrote about *'those who acknowledge no merit in good workes.'* The teaching is laid out in Numbers XI & XII of the *Thirty-Nine 'Articles of Religion,'* which are printed as an appendix to the Anglican Book of Common Prayer.

This publicke Declaration wee have judged necessary to make to all English Catholicks, particularly to those that are of ability, for the discharge of our owne soules, requesting, or rather conjuring all in generall, and everyone in particular by the bowells of our Saviour Jesus Christ to make it their own case, and to have that saying of St. John the Evangelist alwayes before their eyes, *He that shall have the substance of this world, and shall see his brother have neede, and shall shut his bowels from him how doth the Charity of God abide in him?*

6 of October, 1636.　　　　　　　　　　　　　　　　　　　　J.S.
H.M.

　　　　　Permissu Superiorum.

Written in ink in the lower margin is the following:-

'*We underwritten do testify that this letter or Declaration is not feighned but a true and reall thing, and that there is no other end intended thereby, but only to procure due relief for the poor Catholics of London.*'

It is signed by *George Muscott*, Vicar-General in the London District and *John Southcott*, one of the Archdeacons, who were also inmates of the Gatehouse at the time.

SAINT JOHN SOUTHWORTH'S LAST SPEECH[83].

"*Good people, I was born in Lancashire. This is the third time I have been apprehended, and now being to die, I would gladly witness and profess openly my faith for which I suffer. And though my time be short, yet what I shall be deficient in words I hope I shall supply with my blood, which I will most willingly spend to the last drop for my faith. Neither my intent in coming into England, nor practice in England, was to act anything against the secular government. Hither I was sent by my lawful superiors to teach Christ's faith, not to meddle with any temporal affairs. Christ sent His apostles; His apostles their successors; and their successors me. I did what I*

---

[83] Westminster Archives: Transcript of XXX 636, as given by Challoner. There are at least 5 contemporary MS versions of John's last speech, probably all based on the one taken down, (presumably in brachygraphy/shorthand), by the priest standing under the gallows.

was commanded by them, who had power to command me, being ever taught that I ought to obey them in matters ecclesiastical, and my temporal governors in business only temporal.

I never acted nor thought any hurt against the present Protector. I had only a care to do my own obligation and discharge my own duty in saving my own and other men's souls. This, and only this, according to my poor abilities I laboured to perform. I had commission to do it from him, to whom our Saviour in his predecessor St. Peter, gave power to send others to propagate His faith. This is that for which I die, O holy cause! and not for any treason against the laws.

My faith and obedience to my superiors is all the treason charged against me; nay, I die for Christ's law, which no human law, by whomsoever made, ought to withstand or contradict. The law of Christ commanded me to obey

these superiors and this church, saying, whosoever hears them hears Himself. This Church, these superiors of it I obeyed, and for obeying, die. This lesson I have heretofore in my lifetime desired to learn; this lesson I come here to put in practice by dying, being taught it by our Blessed Saviour, both by precept and example. Himself said: "He that will be My disciple, let him take up his cross and follow me." Himself exemplary, practiced what He had recommended to others. To follow His holy doctrine and imitate His holy death, I willingly suffer at present; this gallows (looking up) I look on as His cross, which I gladly take to follow my dear Saviour.

My faith is my crime, the performance of my duty the occasion of my condemnation. I confess I am a great sinner; against God I have offended, but am innocent of any sin against man, I mean the Commonwealth and the present Government. How justly then I die, let them look to who have condemned me. It is sufficient for me that it is God's will; I plead not for myself (I came hither to suffer) but for you poor persecuted Catholics whom I leave behind me.

Heretofore liberty of conscience was pretended as a cause of [civil] war; and it was held a reasonable proposition that all the natives should enjoy it, who should be found to behave themselves as obedient and true subjects. This being so, why should their conscientious acting and governing themselves, according to the faith received from their ancestors, involve them more than all the rest in an universal guilt? — which conscientiousness is the very reason that clears others and renders them innocent.

It has pleased God to take the sword out of the King's hand and put it in the Protector's. Let him remember that he is to administer justice indifferently and without exception to persons. For there is no exception of persons with God whom we ought to resemble. If any Catholics work against the present Government, let them suffer; but why should all the rest who are guiltless (unless conscience be their guilt) be made partakers in a promiscuous punishment with the greatest malefactors? The first rebellion was of the angels; the guilty were cast into hell, the innocent remained partakers of the heavenly blessings."

A GIFT?

Although little is known of John's immediate family a book at Heythrop College entitled *'Discoverie of the Manifold Corruptions of the Holy Scriptures by the Heretiks of our Daies,'* by Gregory Martin, (printed at Rheims in 1582), was probably a parting gift to his man-servant.

The inscription reads:-

'Ex Dono John Southworth who died a martir for the Catholic ffaith — June 28th 1654 — to his servant Jo: Lillie.'

JOHN'S DIVIDED FAMILY

With hindsight, it is hardly surprising that there are more Government records about John than other recusant priests and that the Authorities kept such a close watch on him – because a number of Southworths had been listed as *'obstinate recusants'*, and/or were suspected of rebellion:-

• Sir John Southworth, (who is presumed to have been Saint John's grandfather), was said to be the most well-known recusant in England. He was *'a towarde and tall gentilman,'* a seasoned soldier who had associated himself with a number of treasonous activities and suffered the consequences. Sir John had been excluded from Lancashire during 1584, when worried officials were trying to keep prominent, influential Catholics out of the county.
In 1592 the Rev. Thomas Bell – who had organized 'safe' houses for the Roman Catholic clergy – defected, and laid much information before the Privy Council. The Lord Chief Justice Richard Brereton conducted an intensive drive against persistent recusants. Several Samlesbury residents kept 'open house', where people met and Mass was said, and Sir John was one known to have been *'receiving and sustaining'* seminary priests. His house was ransacked on 21st November, but no priests were found – perhaps a result of the recusants' efficient 'early warning' system. (Of the 800 suspects presented at assizes, only 200 were indicted and of those only eleven paid recusancy fines. Over the next few months the rest of the prisoners were quietly released).

• Sir John's eldest son, Thomas, was reported twice for his hospitality towards seminary priests, and for having a daily Mass at his home. He served a prison sentence, but is known to have conformed c1582/4. It caused dissension with his father, but two of Thomas' sons became Separatists.

- Sir John's daughter Margaret, (whose husband, Bartholomew Hesketh, had befriended Edmund Campion S.J., during a visit to Lancashire before his execution on 1st December 1581), was one of the 'runners' carrying messages, news and warnings within the recusancy network. She was held for a time in the New Fleet Prison, Manchester, as a *'disaffected papist.'*

- Sir John's fourth son, Christopher, was born in 1556 and recruited by Thomas Worthington, an early Lancastrian missioner. Christopher visited Douay with Worthington in 1579, *'against his father's wishes,'* so perhaps Sir John had intended Christopher to go to Oriel College Oxford, where his eldest brother had studied, or maybe he just did not like the missioner. Christopher returned to the continent in 1580 *'without royal approval*[84]*',* studied in Rome and was ordained in 1583.

- Meanwhile, Sir John's second son, (also John), travelled to Rheims[85] in January 1583, with the apparent intention of training for the priesthood and officials noted him as he *'went over from Hythe*[86]*'.* But, according to the Second Douay Diary, after receiving the Tonsure and Minor Orders in 1584, he left at the end of the year and was arrested and imprisoned as soon as he set foot back in England. (The deputy searcher at Dover asked for protection against any suits likely to be urged against him by young John and his two fellow students, *'for staying them at Dover*[87]*').*

---

[84] Haigh, from PRO, SP 12/199, fo. 9, British Museum, Harleian MS 7042, fo. 164. *'By 1593 at least 32 sons of the Lancashire gentry, most from the early recusant families, had gone to the continent without royal approval.'*
[85] The college at Douai relocated to Rheims between 1577 & 1593.
[86] Calendar State Papers – Domestic: Vol. CLVIII: *(Information given to Sec. Walsynham of the passage of priests and recusants from and to England).* Quoted by Southworth & Dudgeon, Part 1.
[87] Calendar State Papers – Domestic, Vol. CLXV, quoted by Southworth & Dudgeon, Part 1. This appears to be the last reference to young John. He is not named in Sir John's will in 1595, so probably predeceased him.

• Christopher was sent on the English Mission in December 1586, but Elizabeth's government was aware of the planned invasion by the Spanish Armada and that the Pope was pledging 1,000,000 gold ducats if it was successful[88]. The country was becoming nervous and Christopher was arrested on his return. When questioned on 2nd March 1587, he stated that he had sojourned in Rome for six years but returned to England *'to recover his health'*. He then admitted that, *'At his coming away he had conference with the pope, as the custom is, who did only persuade him to constancy. But Dr [Cardinal] Allen opposed his coming to England and bade him make probation at Rheims'.* Then, *'about Christmas they took shipping at Boulogne, landed at Dover in the night and so came to London...he was now purposed to ride down to visit his father and friends.'* (Anstruther).

Christopher must have been suspected of being a political activist and he was committed to the *'Compter in Woode Street'*, but c1588, (the year of the Spanish Armada), he was moved to Wisbech Castle, where *'he was very prominent in the disputes, siding with the pro-Jesuit majority.'* He was still there in 1595, when his father made provision in his Will for *'my son Xpofer, being nowe Prisoner in the Castle of Wybyche'* and in December 1598, Christopher was *'deeply charged...upon some matter that hathe of late been dyscovered unto her Majesty of very lewd and dangerous practizes of certaine Jesuits and their adherents*[89]...' He was moved to the Gatehouse, but in 1599 was returned to Wisbeche, from where he escaped in 1600.

Anstruther confirms that Christopher went to earth in Lancashire, where he adopted the alias of *'Thomson'* and worked in the Barton, Pendle and Samlesbury areas. It was whilst he was on his home ground in 1612, that he accused three Samlesbury women of witchcraft:- Jane Southworth, (widow of John, the eldest son of the above Thomas and late nephew of

---
[88] G. Mattingly: *The Defeat of the Spanish Armada*.
[89] Quoted by J.Southworth & A. Dudgeon, part 1: *Acts of Privy Council 1598-99*. Vol.XXIX.

Christopher), and Jennet and Ellen Bierley – apparently taking revenge on them for conforming to the Anglican Church. They were imprisoned and tried at Lancaster, but the evidence of Christopher's main witness, fourteen-years-old Grace Sowerbutts, collapsed in court and the women, (two of whom were Grace's grandmother and aunt respectively), were acquitted.

A fact which does not appear to have been noticed, however, is that other witnesses also committed perjury. They testified that Sir John Southworth used to be so terrified of Jane that he dared not ride past her home and that, although she was his kinsman's wife, (his granddaughter-in-law), she was an evil woman and a witch. But it would appear that Jane was still a ten-year-old girl at *Stonyhurst*[90], (her paternal family's seat), when Sir John died in 1595. (Samlesbury Lower Hall was not made over to Jane and her husband, John Southworth Esq., until 1605).

After the Assizes, Christopher probably made a rapid exit from Samlesbury, but he was never re-captured and *The Foot out of the Snare*[91], (published in April 1624), identifies two Secular *'Fr. Southworths'* – possibly Christopher and Saint John – amongst the 261 priests who either worked in, or frequented London, the previous year.

(Coincidentally, Thomas Worthington – who became President of Douay c1599 – also disgraced the Seculars and was dismissed in 1613. He then joined the Jesuits).

So the close surveillance and sundry records of Saint John's activities would, in part, have resulted from the pursuits of his various relatives. The Authorities would be cautious, suspecting that *Southworth* was still synonymous with *trouble*.

---

[90] Abram's comment about the *'audacious perjury against Jane'* is confirmed by the Wills of Sir Richard Sherburne and Sir John Southworth (Sept 1595).
[91] John Gee – a Puritan who converted to Roman Catholicism, apostatized and then became a Protestant minister.

Perhaps, during his venerable life, John Southworth was hoping to redeem his family's name. The immense distress and ill-will which Christopher would cause – within his family, within Samlesbury and also further afield, would not be easy to erase.

PROBLEMS at SAMLESBURY HIGHER HALL, after the FIRST CIVIL WAR, (1642-1646).

By this time the 6th John Southworth was lord of the Higher Hall moiety of Samlesbury manor and, although there seems to be no record of him having *'taken the field'*, his name appears in the Parliamentarian *'Catalogue of the lords, knights and gentlemen'* whose estates were sequestered in 1646.

A number of the Blackburn Hundred gentry realized that if civil conflict broke out, they and their neighbours would be on opposing sides, so they tried to avert the situation by a friendly understanding amongst themselves. Approximately 200 were Royalists and 100 were Parliamentarians, (S. Bull), but the overtures ended abruptly after Parliament learned of it and thereafter many met only as foes on the battlefield.

It must have put John[6] in an unenviable position – it would appear that his mother, Jane, (who was tried for witchcraft in 1612), may have re-married. There is a marriage licence of 20th September 1623, which refers to an Alexander Rigby and a Jane Southworth, widow, in the parish of Preston/Blackburn/Law Chapel[92]. The Rigbys were close business associates of the Southworths, but Parliamentarians. On the other hand, John's sister-in-law was a Tyldesley and her father, Sir Thomas, was a Roman Catholic Royalist who was also closely involved with the Southworths.

About half of the 700-plus Lancastrian families who claimed 'gentry' status, seem to have remained neutral and John[6]

---

[92] A number of the Southworths were married at Preston. Walton-le-Dale church used to be known as the *'Law'* chapel.'

appears to have been such a one. The Parliamentarians however, considered that those who did not fight for them, were against them and this was probably why, unknown to John, his solicitor described him as *'a papist delinquent'*. (His name appears in the Royalist Composition Papers for 1646).

At the numerous hearings he attended, he pointed out that he had never been convicted for recusancy, or been sequestered and that *'he had and did frequent the church.'* He had also taken the Oath of Abjuration, (a new oath which came into force in 1643). In addition to the denial of papal supremacy *'in this Realm of England,'* the oath demanded that the doctrines of Transubstantiation, Purgatory and Salvation through *'merit by works',* be rejected. Forbidden, too, was the invocation to Crucifixes, Images and the consecrated Host, in line with the 37th, 28th, 22nd, 11th and 12th Articles of the *Thirty-Nine Articles of Religion* respectively, as contained in the Anglican Book of Common Prayer (see p. 100).

Eventually John[6] became *'worn out by long attendances and the necessities of his wife & six children. He therefore chose rather to submit to a fine than any longer lie under the sad condition he was then in…'* Consequently, two-thirds of his real and personal estate was sequestrated[93] by Parliamentary Committee.

It was legalised plunder and if an informer was involved, they were entitled to a shilling in the pound, (one twentieth of the pre-decimal pound), of the value of confiscated property.
John's *'fine was set at £358 18s. 9d',* but five years later, the Lancashire Commissioners were still refusing to 'free' his land. It was not discharged until after the third civil war, (Mar. 1652), when the commissioners added arrears backdated to the previous June[94].

---

[93] Cal. State Papers Dom, (1653-4).
[94] Royalist Composition Papers Lancs. Vol. VI. Part 1-8, pp.115-118.

In addition, John[6] had another financial problem – when he inherited the Hall in-tail from his nephew, (1640), the Mellor estate had been bequeathed to his nieces and he was still disputing ownership. He mortgaged part of the Samlesbury and Mellor estates for £500 and the case dragged on for twenty-six years, until he finally agreed to pay Jane and Elizabeth £318. The litigation, plus sequestration, brought him to the edge of bankruptcy and John still owed Elizabeth £100 – plus interest – when he died in 1676. As records relating to Samlesbury Hall prove, his son Edward had no alternative but to sell the manor and the outstanding money was eventually paid to Elizabeth's grand-daughter.

OLIVER CROMWELL and the FAILED REPUBLIC

Oliver Cromwell-Williams of Huntingdon Esq., (1599–1658), was the only boy of eight surviving children. They were lesser gentry, whose forebears included Thomas Cromwell – Henry VIII's director of the Anglican Reformation.

Although various biographers have found little in his early years to be indicative of his future, they concluded that he was *'a rude, vigorous and unruly youth'* who preferred rough games and sport to the classroom. He was powerfully built and physically strong, a prodigal juvenile who changed to *'zealous righteousness.'*

Oliver would occasionally meet King James when the Royal family stayed with his uncle, Sir Oliver Cromwell and it was said that at three years old, young Oliver quarrelled and fought with the sickly two-year-old Prince Charles, (who had a stammer, speech impediment, suffered from rickets and wore iron boots to strengthen his legs). It was also said, that a clergyman who saved him from drowning had *'lived to repent it publicly.'*

Although Cromwell came from a family which had Puritan leanings, his hatred of episcopacy, Spain and the Church of Rome, (which was then getting into its stride with the Counter-

Reformation), appears to have resulted from his education at the local grammar school, Sydney Sussex College Cambridge (and possibly – briefly – at Lincoln's or Gray's Inn). In each, he came into contact with the *'straitest sect'* of Puritanism. Several of his relatives and friends were at Gray's Inn, (where an unusual number of members opposed Stuart rule), and in later years most of these would hold office under Cromwell. Twenty-two would sign the King's death warrant.

His father died when he was eighteen and it has been suggested that sometime in his earlier life, Cromwell perhaps gained his military knowledge on the Continent during the Thirty Years' War – certainly he was considered to be *'...brave [and] a natural leader [who] had an uncanny ability to read a battle...'*

After marriage (1620), he indulged in country pursuits, kept falcons and entered Parliament, where he particularly concerned himself with matters of religion. Dugdale notes that, *'by his exorbitances at last he so wasted his patrimony,'* he had to sell up. Cromwell considered emigrating to New England, but instead, farmed unsuccessfully at St Ives. Their social status was restored when his uncle bequeathed him a substantial inheritance in 1636.

Sometime during his late twenties or early thirties Cromwell suffered psychiatric problems. For a *'long time'* his doctor and psychiatrist found him to be hallucinating and *'extremely melancholy,'* but he emerged from it *'born again.'*

Convinced of his own righteousness and the *'utter wrongness'* of others, he was the driving force against the Stuart monarchy and episcopacy. His animosity towards bishops was well known and his unacceptable behaviour and *'lack of restraint in language...continually brought him under censure'*. His bad temper *'shocked even seasoned commanders'* in the army.

After entering Parliament in 1640, his scruffy appearance was remarked on and his cousin Hampden responded, *"That slovenly fellow…who hath no ornament in his speech…if we should ever come to have a breach with the King…will be one of the greatest men of England."*

Cromwell was a master of both battles and politics and grasped any opportunity that would implement Puritan/Independent doctrines and principles in the rebellion. He was practical man, had good organizing skills, acted promptly and had an extensive family network which had proved a boon to Pym and the other rebels, who also hated Roman Catholicism.

Britain suffered eleven years of military despotism – the population had never known anything like it. Cromwell's astute political manœuvrings had given him *'more power than any sovereign had possessed, and an army such as no preceding ruler had ever seen much less commanded'*. They were bitter and he *'dare not let the Nation express itself.'*

In January 1655 Cromwell dissolved Parliament. The constitutional experiment had failed and military dictatorship took its place. Ten major-generals were appointed to be regional governors and were given wide-ranging responsibilities for civilian affairs. The country viewed them as repressive, unelected despots, but the generals lacked support – Cromwell's abilities did not always extend to the minutiae of government – in some areas he was a lazy administrator.

An election was called in 1656, but the second Protectorate Parliament was no better than the first. Initially Cromwell *'had entered the civil wars as an avowed champion of liberty against the encroachments of monarchy and ecclesiasticism, but he had now suppressed the freedom of all those not of his own party, in the name of the liberty which he still professed'*. The *'most accomplished soldier-politician in Europe'*, therefore, was not popular.

There were three further attempts on his life after the Gerrard/Vowell plot, but despite strong opposition from Royalists, Presbyterians and Levellers alike, he was offered the Crown in the spring of 1657. Further psychosomatic problems developed – boils on his neck and abdomen, bladder/kidney stones, gout and *'malarial fever'* – but he eventually decided to *'become King in all but name.'*

On 26th June he was sworn into office and, apart from the crowning and anointing ceremonies, the formalities contained most of the elements of a coronation. His robe was of purple velvet lined with ermine, *'being the habit anciently used at the investiture of princes'* and he swore a coronation oath *'to preserve the peace and safety of the people...as Chief Magistrate of these three nations.'* They then handed him the Sword of State and Sceptre. It was the culmination of Cromwell's rise to power.

His first actions as a dictator included the appointment of his son Richard to the Council of State, dissolving the second Protectoral Parliament and bringing about a new Upper Chamber.

This was distasteful to many and Paulucci wrote that the city and the country at large were only kept in subjection by armed force and that *'his assumption of absolute power is so resented that in the general opinion some very important change must befall him ere long'*. Once he assumed absolute authority, Cromwell's life was in real danger and there were frequent reports of assassination plots, both against him and against his immediate supporters. He became paranoid – *"so fearful"*, it was said, that he *"slept behind six locked doors with guards in the intervening rooms."*

Early in 1658 there were four deaths within Cromwell's family, (including his favourite daughter), and he himself fell seriously ill. His long-term ill health had taken their toll and in his latter days, Cromwell is understood to have asked if it was possible to fall from a *'state of grace'?* He must have known that he was hated by the Tories because he had overthrown the monarchy and hated by the Whigs because he had overthrown Parliament.

Cromwell died on 3rd September, the anniversaries of Dunbar and Worcester, having named Richard as his successor. The funeral cost at least £50,000. Official arrangements were for a *lying in state* in Westminster Hall, before his interment at Westminster Abbey on 23rd November, but poor embalming meant that they had to use a life-sized effigy – his decomposing corpse having been buried earlier.

In less than ten years, Royle concluded, Cromwell rose from obscurity to become the most influential man in the country. He was central to the events that led to the overthrow of the monarchy, he had reduced the authority of the Episcopalian clergy, destroyed the Scottish Presbyterians, brought Ireland under control and expelled the Rump.

Abbott opined that Cromwell had been close to the centre of world affairs, but was old before his time, careworn, in poor health and bad-tempered. He also believed that the Lord Protector had privately recognized that the *'peace of the sword'* maintained only an uneasy quiet and he was losing the battle against *'the spirit of the people.'*

RICHARD CROMWELL, the SECOND PROTECTOR

Richard inherited an administration foundering on religious discord and insolvency. The money had run out, the army and navy desperately needed paying and there was an accumulated deficit of almost £2,500,000. In January 1659 Richard recalled Parliament to deal with the financial crisis, but the *Council of Officers* demanded the dissolution of Parliament, the abolition of the Protectorate and a return to Republicanism.

Richard stood down in May, but clashes between the Rump and army continued. Generals Fleetwood and Lambert mounted a coup and appointed a *Committee of Safety*, before Lambert tried to sideline Fleetwood, (Cromwell's son-in-law). The old ways had been destroyed, but the *'un-elected swordsmen'* had failed to establish a new system of government and spent the ensuing years struggling to hang on to power. It is far easier to tear down than to build up and around the country there were repeated calls for the restoration of an elected Parliament.

Two months later there was another unsuccessful Royalist uprising and Charles II was declared King of England in Wrexham.

Fairfax had heard enough. At the beginning of 1660, he emerged from retirement and soldiers flocked to join the veteran commander, as he *'raised Yorkshire'* to restore Parliament. The 'Rump' was revived, republicans expelled and the army brought under civilian control.

George Monck left his settled administration in Scotland, marched south with a large, disciplined army, entered London on 2nd February 1660 and issued an ultimatum to the Rump to dissolve itself and serve writs for a proper election. There were celebrations in the streets, bells rang out, bonfires blazed, soldiers were given drinks and 'rumps' were symbolically roasted. Within six days the 'Long' Parliament was revived and three weeks later they consigned themselves to history.

Monck then contacted the exiled Court and Charles II issued a statement of intent – he would pardon all except the worst of the rebels, confirm the sale of all Royal lands disposed of during the Commonwealth and allow a large measure of religious tolerance. Funds would be raised and army arrears quickly paid. Following the first free election in twenty years, the new Convention Parliament voted for the Kingdom to be governed by *'Kings, Lords and Commons'*, and again there was great rejoicing, as commissioners were despatched to The Hague to bring Charles II home.

Lady Ann Fanshaw reported that Charles and his two brothers were escorted by *'near a hundred brave ships [which sailed] before the wind with the vast cloths and streamers…'* Thirty-two were naval vessels and *'it was a calm evening and moonlit night with everyone in high spirits….So favourable was the wind, that the ships' wherries went from ship to ship to visit their friends, all night long…'* No-one slept and there were *'trumpets and other music'*. There was also great rejoicing as he entered London on 29th May 1660, *'his birth-day, [with] above 20,000 horse and foot brandishing their swords…'*

The Queen returned for a time, but eventually retired to France, where she died in 1669. Royalist exiles too, returned and after Charles' Coronation feast in Westminster Hall, the King's Champion, (Sir Edward Dymoke), appeared – armed and mounted on a charger. He was attended by a page who read out a solemn declaration:

> *"If any dare deny Charles Stewart to be the lawful King of England, here is a Champion who will fight with him."*

Parliament decided which of the fifty's worst offenders would be hanged, drawn and quartered for treason and which would be beheaded or hanged, only. Five of the forty-one regicides, (including Cromwell and Ireton), had previously died. These were exhumed and publicly displayed in Westminster Hall.

General Montrose, (an unswerving Royalist and *'one of the greatest of the Royalist military leaders'*), was re-interred in the High Kirk of Saint Giles, Edinburgh, with great pomp and ceremony. Major-

General Monck was made Duke of Albemarle, and granted the honor of Clitheroe in 1661. He was, therefore, the Lord paramount of Samlesbury. Marmaduke Langdale[95] was knighted for his services to the deceased King, Fairfax received a Royal pardon, army arrears were paid, the *'Solemn League and Covenant'* statute was repealed and the Church of England re-established.

Whilst the majority of soldiers returned to civilian life, others joined garrisons in Ireland, Scotland, or abroad and became the foundation of the modern British Army. As soon as funds permitted, Charles also planned to expand the *'New Model Navy'*, which had emerged in 1649. (Henry VIII had built more warships than any contemporary European monarch and Elizabeth and Charles I had continued the investment). Between 1649 and 1651, Cromwell added a further forty-two ships to the thirty-nine in service, which cost over £2,000,000 – profits from the forfeiture of the Royal estates – and planned a further 200, for both commerce and defence. The largest of the 156 warships in service, were all more powerful than anything in Europe.

Prince Rupert, (1619-1682), was appointed to the Privy Council, became the first Governor of the Canadian Hudson's Bay Company (1670), and took a great interest in the improvement of ordnance. His invention of a modified form of brass became known as 'prince's metal' and he was a founder-member of the Royal Society. He also held posts in the navy and admiralty and on his death, was given a State Funeral and buried in Westminster Abbey.

The civil wars cost England and Wales dearly and the emotional aftermath must have been very great. Figures suggest that in total 85,000 soldiers died, (50,000 being Royalists) and a further

---

[95] Marmaduke's great grandson married Dorothy Walmesley, née Dandy, who set up the Langdale Charity in Samlesbury.

40,000 non-combatants were victims of siege warfare, rape, murder, plague and other disease. In addition, over 4,000 surviving Royalists were impoverished by heavy fines, when their land and possessions were sequestrated.

Estimates of Scottish military casualties have been put at 28,000, with the loss of a further 15,000 non-combatants; and Ireland fared even worse – death through warfare was estimated to be at least 192,000.

The republican rebellion failed, but the British civil wars overturned an ancient order, in which the power of the sovereign had cascaded down, (through land grants etc.), to the aristocratic class, who let it to those lower down the social scale, until it reached the common man. When the order of Sovereign, Lords and Commons was revived, the partnership became better balanced and our Constitutional monarchy has stood the test of time.

BIBLIOGRAPHY

A History of Blackburn, Town and Parish: William A. Abram, 1877.

A History of the Southworths of Samlesbury, Part 1: John Southworth & Anne Dudgeon, 1994.

A Procession of Lancashire Martyrs and Confessors: Fr. J.A. Myerscough, SJ.

Blackburn, Lancashire. Chronological Notes of Prominent Historical Events: Wm. Durham.

Brindle Historical Society.

Civil War: Trevor Royle, 2004.

Defending the Faith: Mr. Bernard Loffler.

Guide to the Crypt of the Martyrs of Tyburn: Tyburn Convent.

London in the Time of the Stuarts: Besant.

Memoirs: Butler MSS..

Memoirs of Missionary Priests: Bishop Richard Challoner.

Oral tradition.

Preston 1648: Dr. Richard Holmes.

Reformation and Resistance in Tudor Lancashire: Christopher Haigh, 1975.

John Southworth Priest and Martyr. Fr. E.E. Reynolds, 1962.

Saints of the Isles: *John Southworth*, Fr. Michael Archer. CTS. AD.2010.

Saint John Southworth: Fr. R.J. Whitfield. (CTS. AD.1970).

Saint John Southworth, The Parish Priest of Westminster: Fr. N. Schofield & Fr. G. Skinner, 2012.

Staging the World: Shakespeare: J. Bate & D. Thornton.

The Basilikon Doron of King James VI. (Ed. Jas. Craigie), Edinburgh, Scottish Texts Society, 1944, 7-8.

The Civil War in Lancashire: Stephen Bull.

The Defeat of the Spanish Armada: G. Mattingly: 1961.

The Foot out of the Snare: J. Gee, pub.1624.

The Life of Blessed John Southworth: Fr. Albert B. Purdie., 1930.

The Popish Royall Favourite: William Prynne.

The Seminary Priests: Fr. Godfrey Anstruther, O.P..

The Third Douai Diary.

The Wonderful Discovery of Witches in the Countie of Lancaster: Thomas Potts, 1613.

The Writings and Speeches of Oliver Cromwell: Volumes I, II & III: ed. by W.C. Abbott, 1945.

White King – the Tragedy of Charles I: Leanda de Lisle